# ROUTLEDGE LIBRARY EDITIONS: LIBRARY AND INFORMATION SCIENCE

Volume 8

# AUTHOR'S GUIDE TO JOURNALS IN LIBRARY & INFORMATION SCIENCE

# AUTHOR'S GUIDE TO JOURNALS IN LIBRARY & INFORMATION SCIENCE

Edited by
NORMAN D. STEVENS AND NORA B. STEVENS

LONDON AND NEW YORK

First published in 1982 by The Haworth Press, Inc.

This edition first published in 2020
by Routledge
2 Park Square, Milton Park, Abingdon, Oxon OX14 4RN

and by Routledge
52 Vanderbilt Avenue, New York, NY 10017

*Routledge is an imprint of the Taylor & Francis Group, an informa business*

© 1982 The Haworth Press, Inc.

All rights reserved. No part of this book may be reprinted or reproduced or utilised in any form or by any electronic, mechanical, or other means, now known or hereafter invented, including photocopying and recording, or in any information storage or retrieval system, without permission in writing from the publishers.

*Trademark notice*: Product or corporate names may be trademarks or registered trademarks, and are used only for identification and explanation without intent to infringe.

*British Library Cataloguing in Publication Data*
A catalogue record for this book is available from the British Library

ISBN: 978-0-367-34616-4 (Set)
ISBN: 978-0-429-34352-0 (Set) (ebk)
ISBN: 978-0-367-43411-3 (Volume 8) (hbk)
ISBN: 978-0-367-43412-0 (Volume 8) (pbk)
ISBN: 978-1-00-300300-7 (Volume 8) (ebk)

**Publisher's Note**
The publisher has gone to great lengths to ensure the quality of this reprint but points out that some imperfections in the original copies may be apparent.

**Disclaimer**
The publisher has made every effort to trace copyright holders and would welcome correspondence from those they have been unable to trace.

# AUTHOR'S GUIDE TO JOURNALS
## in library & information science

Edited by
Norman D. Stevens, Ph.D.
Nora B. Stevens, M.L.S.

THE HAWORTH PRESS, NEW YORK

© 1982 by The Haworth Press. All rights reserved. No part of this work may be reproduced or utilized in any form or by any means, electronic or mechanical, including photocopying, microfilm and recording, or by any information storage and retrieval system, without permission in writing from the publisher.

The Haworth Press, 28 East 22 Street, New York, New York 10010

**Library of Congress Cataloging in Publication Data**

Stevens, Norman D
   Author's guide to journals in library and information science.

   (Author's guide to journals series)
   Bibliography: p.
   Includes index.
   1. Library science—Periodicals—Directories. 2. Information science—Periodicals—Directories. 3. Library science—Authorship. 4. Information science—Authorship. I. Stevens, Nora B., joint author. II. Title. III. Series.
Z666.S84                           020.5                           80-20964
ISBN 0-917724-13-5

Printed in the United States of America

## CONTENTS

| | |
|---|---|
| Introduction | 1 |
|     *Table One: Questionnaire* | 5 |
|     *Table Two: Information Included for Each Journal* | 8 |
| Writing for Publication | 11 |
| Selected Bibliography | 23 |
| Abbreviations Used: Abstracting and Indexing Services | 27 |
| Abbreviations Used: Style Manuals | 30 |
| ALPHABETICAL LISTING OF JOURNALS | 31 |
| Other Journals | 173 |
| Association, Keyword, and Subject Index | 178 |

# INTRODUCTION

*Purpose of This Guide*

The basic purpose of this guide is to assist prospective authors in preparing and submitting articles for publication by providing information about the policies and practices of the major journals in library and information science. It is, first of all, important to know which journal may be most interested in a particular topic or most suitable for the submission of a particular article. While there are some basic requirements for preparing and submitting material for publication, each journal has its own standards and its own idiosyncracies. The author who prepares an article in conformity with the requirements of a particular journal not only may have a somewhat better chance of having that article accepted but also may save considerable time and effort. And by knowing more about the policies and practices of a journal, the prospective author can know what to expect in his or her dealings with that journal. This guide is intended to help in all of those respects.

This guide also provides general guidance of a more personal and subjective nature in the essay on writing for publication, and it contains a selected bibliography, with its own brief introduction, of articles related to the general topic of professional writing and the library press.

*Criteria for Selection*

For many years the professional library press was relatively small and stable. There were a few standard major journals, a larger number of local and state journals and newsletters, and a handful of specialized journals. For reasons that are not entirely clear the past few years have seen a proliferation of specialized journals each offering much wider opportunities to the prospective author. There are now probably well over 500 journals in the field of library and information science. It would be neither possible nor desirable to include all of those titles in this guide. Many of them, particularly the state and local journals, are intended to serve, both in terms of readership and generally authorship, a limited audience of professional librarians in a certain geographic area. Many of those journals, as well as some specialized newsletters of wider geographic interest, consist primarily of news and informational items and thus offer somewhat limited opportunities for the individual author. In any case it does not seem necessary to include them in a publication intended for a more general, national audience. Those journals do, however, offer good opportunities for the beginning author, who can prepare news and informational items as well as serve as a regular contributor or even as an editor. Practice in writing for publication, no matter how brief or specific the material and no matter how limited the audience, provides good experience and can help overcome the initial difficulties that the beginning writer often experiences.

Basically this guide includes the major American, Canadian, English, and international professional journals that solicit, accept, and publish articles in the field of library and information science and in some related fields and specialties.

The selection in the field of librarianship itself was relatively simple. Perhaps the major exclusion, apart from the local and state journals and a number of newsletters, has been the many foreign journals published in English. While many of those welcome and include articles of relevance from American authors, they are designed more for native authors and readers and tend to accept and include material by foreign authors only if it is directly related to some aspect of librarianship in the country in which it is published. Since the number of American authors likely to be writing that kind of material is quite limited, most foreign journals in English, and all not in English, have been excluded. Journals of a broader international nature, however, when not as restrictive in their audience or their content, have been included.

In addition to the more general library journals there are a number of specialized ones, which offer opportunities for authors with particular subject or professional specialties. The number of prospective authors, and indeed the number of readers, may be somewhat limited but often these journals are more receptive to submissions from a prospective author, especially one who has not previously been published, writing about a particular topic of special interest to the editor and the readership.

The field of information science presented somewhat greater problems in the selection process. Here almost all local, state, and regional journals, specialized journals, and foreign journals have been excluded. Only more general titles that seem to offer a potential opportunity for the prospective author with a library and information science background have been included. Those general titles that seem to be for computer specialists, engineers, information scientists, and technicians have been excluded. The dividing line is a thin one; in cases where there seems to be any question, a journal has been included rather than excluded.

Librarians have a number of related interests that go beyond their primary interest in librarianship and information science. Specialized subject fields that are either a part of, closely allied to, or of particular interest to librarians include: archives, audio-visual work, bibliography, book collecting, book publishing, and children's literature. Representative major journals from those fields have been included in this guide. But many other specialized subject journals for which librarians might write have been excluded. The law librarian writing on a legal subject, for example, or sometimes writing on aspects of law librarianship of interest to a wider legal audience, may well wish to submit an article to any one of a number of legal journals. Information about the editorial and publishing practices of such journals can be found elsewhere, including other guides in this series.

A number of library journals in the alternative press area have been included, even though they are not looking for the traditional library journal article, because they offer unusual and unique opportunities often lacking in the other professional literature. These journals tend to be more receptive to the author who is younger or who has different, innovative, and provocative points of view.

*Content of the Guide*

The description of each journal in this guide is based almost entirely on information supplied by the current editor and/or publisher in response to a questionnaire sent out in late 1979 (Table One). The organization of this information is described and explained in detail in Table Two. Four major areas of interest are covered. First basic factual information is provided about the editorial and subscription addresses, price, frequency, and so forth. Much of that information is readily available elsewhere and may not be absolutely essential to the prospective author; but it seems to be such a fundamental part of the nature of librarianship to be interested in and to use such information that it has been included. Next some general information about the editorial policy, audience, and topical interests of the journal is provided. This will help the prospective author determine whether the article he or she has written, or is thinking about writing, is appropriate for submission to a particular journal. Next information is provided about some of the mechanical aspects of the preparation of an article to meet the particular requirements of a specific journal. Time and effort can be saved for all if, for example, the right number of copies prepared in the right format are submitted initially. Finally basic information about the editorial and publication policies and practices of each journal is included to enable the prospective author to determine what to expect in terms of the handling and eventual publication of his or her work.

## Other Publishing Opportunities

Much of a librarian's work involves bibliographies, guides, indexes, and other compilations and reference tools. Thus it is only natural that librarians often engage in the production of such works either as a part of their work or as a natural adjunct to it. Many of these tools are most appropriately published within the individual library but not all libraries take the fullest advantage of modern printing capabilities to produce these publications in an attractive, durable, and often saleable format. They should be encouraged to do so. Sometimes such compilations, if they are of a general topical interest that goes beyond the individual library, may be appropriately published, if they are brief, in a subject journal, or, if they are longer and more substantial, as a separate book publication either by a subject or professional library publisher.

Encouraging, at least from the perspective of the would-be author, is the fact that whereas ten years ago there were only two or three specialized library publishers, there are now an increasing number of such publishers so that the opportunities are much greater. It has not been possible, within the scope of this guide, to incorporate information about book publishers. In any case, unlike journal articles, few books in a professional field are written on speculation. The process usually involves the suggestion of an idea, and subsequently the preparation and submission of a detailed outline and perhaps even a sample chapter, to a publisher, with considerable negotiation and discussion before a contract is signed. The would-be book author is best advised to contact and work with a publisher long before he begins to produce the manuscript.

Modern printing capabilities also offer the prospective author excellent, and inexpensive, self-publishing opportunities. It is relatively simple, for example, to initiate a specialized journal or newsletter, either within a library setting or independently, which allows an author, and others with similar interests, to express their views. Self-publishing is a contemporary phenomenon that is likely to be increasingly significant for the literature of librarianship.

All librarians need to be aware of and alert to new and different publishing opportunities. The technology of publication and the economics of publication are undergoing rapid change. Electronic journals, for example, may soon be here on a widespread basis and they will offer new publishing opportunities, new conditions, and new limitations. We must adapt to and make the best use of those opportunities.

# TABLE ONE
## QUESTIONNAIRE

**GENERAL INFORMATION**

1. What is the correct address for submitting subscription orders? _____

2. What is the cost of an annual subscription (in U.S. dollars):

   Individuals ( ) Institutions ( ) Other ( ) _____

3. What are the name(s) of your current editors? _____

4. What is the frequency of your journal? _____

5. What is the approximate circulation of your journal? _____

6. In which indexing or abstracting services is your journal covered or listed (as of information provided Fall 1979)? _____

7. What is the ISSN of your journal? _____

**BRIEF HISTORY**

8. Date of your first publication: _____

9. Previous title(s), if any: _____

10. Other historical information: _____

**CHARACTER AND NATURE**

11. General statement of editorial policy: _____

12. Your intended audience: _____

13. Is your journal affiliated with or sponsored by any society? _____

    (if so, please indicate): _____

*Continued next page*

14. What kinds of articles or topics are of particular interest to your journal? _____

15. What topics do you frequently receive but wish you hadn't? _____

16. What types of articles are most likely to be accepted for publication in your journal? Please indicate with numbers in rank order of perference:
( ) research articles  ( ) theoretical articles  ( ) review articles  ( ) case studies
( ) unsolicited book reviews  ( ) commentaries  ( ) OTHER---(please specify) _____

17. What special features do you publish (especially ones for which you may solicit contributions)? _____

18. What professional and/or general book reviews do you publish? (please indicate which, if either, you normally publish; and if you publish reviews, how one becomes a reviewer). _____

## MANUSCRIPT SUBMISSION

19. Is a cover letter desirable? ( ) Yes ( ) No

20. Is an abstract required (if so, please indicate length and requirements): _____

21. How many copies of a manuscript do you require for review purposes? _____

22. What are your format requirements? _____

23. What are your style requirements?
( ) standard style sheet or format (if so, please specify): _____
( ) house style sheet or format (if so, please indicate if copy is available to prospective authors): _____
( ) other requirements (if any): _____

24. Will you send a copy of your journal manuscript requirements on request to a prospective author? ( ) Yes ( ) No

25. Do you as matter of policy seek or encourage the submission of one or two "student papers" every year for publication? ( ) Yes ( ) No

26. What is the approximate word length of most articles accepted for publication in your journal? _____

27. Do you have any authorship restrictions as to who may publish in your journal (e.g., society members only, etc.)? ( ) No
( ) Yes. Restricted to: _____

## DISPOSITION OF MANUSCRIPTS

28. Manuscript receipt acknowledge (please note any requirements): _____

29. How long does it usually take from the time a manuscript is received until the author is notified whether it has been accepted or rejected? _____

30. Is your journal refereed? _____

31. What type of review procedure do you use? ( ) Editorial Board
( ) External Review ( ) Other: _____

32. Do you indicate the reasons why a manuscript is rejected? _____

33. Do you provide criticisms of rejected manuscripts? _____

## PUBLICATION PRACTICES

34. Approximately what percentage of manuscripts are accepted for publication? _____

35. How long does it usually take from the time an article is accepted until it is published? _____

36. Do you have an early publication option? ( ) Yes ( ) No

37. Does your journal have any page charges? ( ) Yes ( ) No

38. Are the exclusive rights to the article retained by journal between acceptance and publication?
( ) Yes ( ) No

39. What is the normal extent of editorial revisions?
( ) heavy ( ) medium ( ) light

40. Are proofs sent to the author for correction? _____
(if so, please note any requirements): _____

41. Copyright for initial serial publication is held by: ( ) author
( ) journal ( ) publisher ( ) material not copyrighted
( ) other (please specify): _____

42. Copyright for republication is held by: ( ) author ( ) journal
( ) publisher ( ) other (please specify): _____

43. Is there a fee paid for articles? (if so, please indicate normal rate and when payment is made): _____

44. How many reprints does the author receive free of charge? _____

45. How many reprints are available for purchase? _____
(please indicate cost and conditions): _____

46. Do you require that the author purchase reprints? ( ) Yes ( ) No

47. Are reprints available by any other method of payment?
(if so, please indicate): _____

## TABLE TWO
## INFORMATION INCLUDED FOR EACH JOURNAL

JOURNAL TITLE: The correct, current title of the journal.

SUBSCRIPTION ADDRESS: The correct address for placing a subscription.

PRICE: The cost of an individual subscription in American dollars unless noted otherwise. It should be noted that a number of journals also have special rates for association members, libraries, students, etc. Since it has not been possible because of space limitations to include all possible subscription rates in this guide, it is advisable to check a recent issue of a journal before ordering, or to write to the subscription address for more complete information.

FREQUENCY: The number of times per year the journal is published.

CIRCULATION: The size of the journal's circulation.

AFFILIATION: The name of any association or organization thatis connected with the publication of the journal.

INDEXED/ABSTRACTED: A listing of the indexing and abstracting services that cover the journal as given by the editor or listed in the journal.

MANUSCRIPT ADDRESS: The correct, current address for the submission of manuscripts. Many library journals are dependent upon volunteer editors who change with some frequency. If in doubt it may be best to attempt to verify this information from a recent issue of the journal.

EDITORIAL POLICY: A brief statement of the general areas that are of primary interest is indicated by the journal's current editor.

AUDIENCE: Those for whom the journal is intended.

PREFERRED TOPICS: A list of specific topics that the current editor indicates are of interest.

INAPPROPRIATE TOPICS: Specific topics that are clearly outside the scope of the journal.

FEATURES: Special sections of the journal that are published on a regular basis, especially those for which contributions may be sought.

REVIEWS: An indication of whether or not the journal regularly publishes reviews of professional and/or trade publications.

## Table Two: Information Included for Each Journal

STUDENT PAPERS: Whether papers written by students as part of their educational program are published by the journal.

RESTRICTIONS: Whether or not there are any limitations on who may publish in the journal (e.g., only members of the society).

COVER LETTER: Whether or not the editor encourages prospective authors to include a brief cover letter describing their manuscript as part of the submission.

ABSTRACT: Whether or not prospective authors are required to submit an abstract of their manuscript as part of the submission; if so, the length of that abstract in number of words.

NUMBER OF COPIES: The number of copies of a manuscript which should be submitted.

LENGTH: The general length of articles, normally given in terms of the number of words, that is considered appropriate for the journal.

STYLE: The style manual, if any, that prospective authors are expected to follow in preparing a manuscript for the journal.

INSTRUCTION FORM: Whether the journal has a specific form it will send prospective authors on request describing its requirements, including style, for the preparation and submission of manuscripts.

FORMAT: A brief statement of the general requirements of the form in which manuscripts should be submitted. The term *Standard* indicates that manuscripts should be typed double-spaced on one side of good quality white 8-1/2 inch x 11 inch paper with ample margins on both sides.

ACKNOWLEDGED: An indication of whether the journal normally acknowledges the receipt of a manuscript, and of any special requirements (i.e., enclosure of a self-addressed stamped envelope) for acknowledgment.

NOTIFICATION TIME: How long it normally takes between the receipt of a manuscript and the notification to the author of its acceptance or rejection.

REVIEW PROCESS: An indication of who is involved in the decision to publish a manuscript, including the use of an editorial board and/or external reviewers.

CRITICISM: Whether the journal normally provides suggestions for improving or revising a manuscript that is being rejected.

ACCEPTANCE RATE: The editor's estimate of the percentage of the manuscripts received by the journal that are actually published by it.

PUBLICATION TIME LAG: The editor's estimate of the usual interval between the time an article is accepted for publication and its actual publication.

REVISION: The extent, in general terms, to which the journal normally makes revisions in manuscripts that it has accepted for publication.

PROOFS: Whether the author normally receives proofs of his article and is expected to participate in the correction of those proofs.

EARLY PUBLICATION OPTION: Whether the journal will publish an article sooner than usual if special payment is made for that service.

PAGE CHARGES: Whether the journal requires the author, or author's institution, to help subsidize publication of an article, after it has already been determined that the article will be published, by the payment of a portion of the publication costs assessed on a per page basis; and, if so, the amount of those page charges.

COPYRIGHT POLICY: Whether or not material published in the journal is normally copyrighted, and, if it is, a general statement of who holds the initial copyright.

FEE: The amount of the payment, if any, normally made to authors for published articles.

REPRINTS: The policy of the journal regarding the distribution and sale of reprints of articles, or of copies of the issue of the journal in which an article appears, to the author.

## WRITING FOR PUBLICATION

The basic purpose of this guide is to provide specific, objective information about the editorial and publishing policies and practices of the major journals in the field of library and information science. Writing for publication is an art, however, and any guide of this kind, if it is to be successful, should also supply the author with other, less objective, aid and assistance. The purpose of this essay then is to provide the prospective author wishing to prepare and submit material to a professional journal in the field of library and information science with some ideas and opinions about how to go about preparing an article for publication. This essay is based, in large part, on my own experience in writing for publication over a period of more than twenty years. It reflects, therefore, my own personal opinions, including what has been learned through experience about the policies and practices of journal editors and publishers. It is also based, in part, on the specific experience gained through my direction of the work of the New England Academic Librarians' Writing Seminar, a project sponsored by the Council on Library Resources, from 1977 through 1979. That Seminar was intended to assist a small group of professional librarians in improving their writing skills by preparing material for publication. Finally this essay is based also on a presentation of the work of that Seminar made to a meeting of the College and University Library Section of the Connecticut Library Association in 1978, on a discussion of the issues surrounding writing for publication with the professional staff of the Library of the State University of New York at Albany in 1979, and on an essay, also entitled "Writing for Publication" that is listed in the bibliography below, that grew out of the work of that Seminar.

### *Why Do We Write?*

In order to put my ideas and opinions about how to approach writing an article for publication into perspective, it is first necessary to look briefly at the question of why it is that we, as librarians engaged in a professional activity, feel it necessary to write for publication.

Like most human processes the process of writing for professional publication is a complex one. Many factors enter into the question of why librarians do and should write for publication. Certainly many of us are engaged in jobs that require a considerable amount of written communication and the time and energy required for work-related writing may effectively preclude any idea of writing for publication. Yet, of course, the writing that we do at work tends to be less organized and less precise, as well as of a somewhat different character, than that we do for publication partly because it is not subject ordinarily to any real editorial scrutiny. Certainly the more careful task of writing for publication should help improve writing skills and techniques generally, and should result in a better product for the letters, memos, and reports that are a part of our work routines.

It is easy to take a cynical view of why we write for publication, ascribing to librarians, and especially academic librarians, simply an effort to become engaged in writing in an attempt to emulate our faculty counterparts who are caught up in what to some seems to be a meaningless effort to publish in order not to perish in their academic careers. To some degree, and in some instances, that view may be true but it needs to be examined carefully.

First of all the idea that *all* faculty members are frantically engaged in research and publication is a misleading one. Among other things investigated by Ladd and Lipset in an extensive survey of American faculty members in 1977 was the extent to which they published scholarly articles.* Those findings showed that in the social sciences and the humanities roughly one-third of the faculty had not published any scholarly articles and only about another one-third had published five or more articles. With the exception of the biological sciences, law, and medicine, all of which showed higher rates of publication, the faculty in most other disciplines were performing at approximately the same, if not lower, levels of activity. Obviously there are underlying differences, such as age and tenure status, that were not reported on in that survey. Nevertheless it is clear that we, as librarians, ought not to feel that we all have to write scholarly articles for publication in order to emulate the faculty. On the other hand a similar survey taken among librarians would, in all likelihood, show a somewhat lower level of publishing activity than that reported for almost all faculty members; although I suspect that recent years have shown a marked increase in the number of librarians engaged in writing for publication. Perhaps the observation can be made that while we do not *all* have to write for publication, an overall improvement in our collective efforts, in terms of both quantity and quality, might be desirable.

---

*See chart prepared by Everett C. Ladd and Seymour Lipset in *The Chronicle of Higher Education* November 28, 1977 p. 2.

It is also essential to understand that research and publication by faculty and other professionals is not always a mindless process engaged in simply for the sake of achieving promotion and tenure or some other tangible reward. There are valid reasons why institutions and professions emphasize research and publication. Those reasons are equally valid for us as librarians in the context of our work.

Surely we must recognize that one of our most important roles is in the preservation and transfer of information and knowledge. Our society, and especially our profession, is built around information and the use of information. It follows, therefore, that the preparation and publication of written information about librarianship is important; it forms the primary intellectual basis for our profession and our work. Surely as a profession we would not be where we are today in the provision of library service without the solid intellectual base provided by our predecessors through their writings and publications. We need, and must have, this kind of exchange and preservation of ideas through the written word. Some of us must, therefore, engage in this kind of activity.

There is now an increasingly high and valid expectation that a librarian must maintain a strong record of professional growth and development over the span of a long career. No matter how good one's intentions may be, a librarian cannot just teach or practice what was learned as a student and expect to continue to serve effectively over a long period of time. That is, of course, especially true with the dramatic changes that are occurring in librarianship. No matter how good one's efforts may be, it is difficult, if not impossible, to maintain an adequate understanding of the developments in librarianship, or indeed any field, over a period of time only by reading what others think and have done, by attending meetings, or by participating in continuing education activities. The kind of professional growth and development that is most needed and most valuable can best be achieved by the detailed immersion in research, or other intensive scholarly activity, of the kind that normally results in writing for publication. The process of putting one's ideas and observations into writing, and of subjecting them to the critical process of publication, is an essential aspect of a strong program of professional growth and development both for an individual and for a profession.

Then, of course, there are a large number of personal factors to be considered. No one writes just for the sake of writing no matter how strong the external motivations may seem to be. Most writing, and certainly the best and most satisfying writing, is done by individuals who have a keen interest in an idea, and who have a strong desire to put their thoughts into a form that can be shared with, appreciated by, or challenged by others. The self-motivation that leads one to write for publication, and the self-satisfaction that comes with publication, are key elements in the process.

Many of us at times, and even some of us all the time, may write for publication for reasons of personal vanity. It may be an attempt to impress our colleagues, friends, or relatives with our wisdom and importance. It may simply be a vain wish to see our own name in print attached to an important piece of research. Or it may be an attempt to achieve a kind of personal immortality by leaving behind publications that someday, long after we are dead, others may read and use.

On the whole, however, I believe that we should largely discount the more cynical views of why librarians write for publication. Writing for publication is an extremely important aspect of librarianship for institutional, personal, and professional reasons.

*How To Begin*

Writing an article for publication in a professional journal is generally viewed as a difficult task requiring special skills. It is unquestionably a difficult task; writing involves hard intellectual work and requires the expenditure of considerable time and effort to produce a finished product of quality. It does not necessarily require special skills; writing involves little more than the use of basic language skills and a good deal of common sense.

How does one approach writing an article for publication? Begin by selecting a topic that you have thought about and understand. Know what others have already written about the subject. Have a clear idea of what it is that you want to say that has not already been said. This initial step of identifying a subject and organizing in your mind the ideas which you want to present is perhaps the most difficult one, but it is an essential one. Incidentally there is no question but what the most effective writing is done when an author is keenly interested in an idea or subject and is seeking to convey his interest and enthusiasm to others.

Next, and still before you actually begin to write, gather together all of the information that you will need. Review that information carefully. Whether what you want to write is based on opinion, practice, or research, it is essential to have a reasonable body of work and ideas as a starting point. If, for example, your article is to be based on research, both the research and your analysis of the results should be relatively complete before you start to write. Obviously it is neither possible nor desirable to be totally prepared. Inevitably as you translate ideas and facts into words, new thoughts and the need for additional facts that require further investigation will occur to you.

To a considerable degree the mechanics of writing are a matter of personal preference but there are some guidelines, which while they may seem mechanistic and simple, may also be helpful. If they seem obvious it is because they are. No one is likely to find fault with these basic suggestions but, paradoxically, some of them may be impossible to achieve. Everyone will agree, for example, that papers intended for publication should be grammatically correct, but that will not prevent many writers, as almost every journal editor can attest, from writing papers that contain numerous grammatical errors. The point is only that in writing for publication you should pay particular attention to the common sense details.

Writing can be accomplished best in a quiet place and when you have a reasonable period of time in which to work. Before you start to write make sure again that you are fully prepared to do so. Have one clearly defined topic in mind to write on. As you progress, be certain that you stick to it. It may help to assign a descriptive working title to your proposed piece. It often helps to attempt to express concisely, in a kind of rough abstract, the general ideas that are to be presented in the article. Next produce an outline, or at least write down in some rough but organized form the facts, ideas, and opinions that you want to include. This should be a working document intended to serve as a guideline in the writing process as well as to serve as a means for evaluating the finished product to make sure that it covers all that you intended. Neither the rough abstract nor the outline, no matter how well organized it may be, should be followed in slavish detail for in writing new ideas and new areas to be covered inevitably appear and need to be incorporated.

Having done all of that preparation, you should at last be ready to start writing. The equipment that you use is entirely a matter of personal preference but here again common sense should prevail. Through trial and error, for example, discover how your thought processes work in relationship to the tools you are using. If your thought processes are slow and methodical, use a pen or pencil rather than a typewriter which tends to be a far more rapid means of writing.

Write a draft. Try to be as well organized as possible in doing so but don't agonize so much over the selection of particular words or phrases that you become bogged down and accomplish nothing. Once a first version of the article is on paper, a substantial portion of the task is accomplished. But do not be satisfied with your first version no matter how meticulously it has been constructed. Read what you have written; think about it; put it aside; think about it some more; come back to it; read it again; and then start making revisions.

It may be helpful to share a semi-final draft with others to see if they understand what it is you are trying to say. If you do so, be prepared to accept, or at least consider, their criticism. An attachment to your words once they have been put down on paper that prevents you from making changes and revisions is a mistake. To write an acceptable paper should take several drafts unless you are a remarkably accomplished writer. The total amount of time required will vary greatly from individual to individual and from subject to subject depending on many factors, including experience, but for a beginner it may well take as much as twenty hours to produce a five-page, double-spaced, typewritten paper. The time required, incidentally, is likely to increase geometrically with the length and complexity of the article.

Papers intended for publication should be concise, grammatically correct, and intelligible. Jargon should be avoided at all costs, as should obscure references and unusual language. While you should express your ideas clearly and forcefully and should attempt to be original, it does not pay, especially for a beginning author, to adopt an idiosyncratic style. Editors, and readers, expect material to be written in a standard format and style unless you are an exceptionally gifted, or an established, author. Put your ideas in a logical order and do not digress. Make sure as you write the final version that your research has been thorough, that your facts are correct, that your citations are adequate and accurate, and that the ideas expressed represent what you want to say in a way that others will understand.

*Submitting a Manuscript*

Again it should be emphasized that the purpose of the main section of this guide is to provide detailed, factual information about editorial and publishing practices of individual journals so that the prospective author can determine what he or she needs to know about submitting a manuscript for publication to an individual journal and about seeing it through to the finished product. In submitting a manuscript for publication it is important to tailor the submission to the requirements of a particular journal, obtaining the necessary information either from this guide, or a similar publication, or directly from the editor or publisher.

To provide some general guidance, however, I have attempted to make some comments and observations about that process. These comments describe what one might generally expect to find in the way of editorial and publishing policies and practices in the field of library and information science. It should be noted that these observations are not based on a statistical analysis of the information derived from the questionnaires submitted to the editors and publishers (Table One). Rather they are based on a sense of the general content of the responses to those questionnaires and on personal observation based on dealings with a number of editors and publishers over a period of time. In dealing with a particular journal it is essential to confirm or deny these more general observations by checking the entry for that journal in the main section of the guide.

First of all the language and tone of an article should be appropriate for the subject, your approach, and the intended audience. Since the latter is largely shaped by the journal, it pays to have in mind which journal, or perhaps journals, you plan to submit an article to before you put the work into final form. Typed double-spaced manuscripts done on one side of clean 8-1/2 inch x 11 inch white bond paper with ample margins (at least 1 inch on all sides) are generally satisfactory. But again these and other details, such as the number of copies to be submitted, the need for an abstract, the location of the author's name, the form of the cover page, and so forth, are all matters of individual journal policy. In some cases journals specify that a particular style manual is to be used as a guide in the preparation of a manuscript and some journals have information sheets for authors that give additional information about their requirements. That information is useful although it is my impression that the style manual requirements are not rigidly adhered to.

Most professional library journals are not refereed; that is, articles submitted for publication are not normally submitted anonymously to one or more individuals knowledgeable in the field before a decision on publication is made. Refereed journals are more common in the field of information science and are standard practice with scientific journals. With most library journals it is more common for the editor, and/or some members of his staff or editorial advisory board, to decide what is, or is not, published. To the prospective author the differences in these approaches may be slight. Presumably the refereeing process is more rigorous and objective and it is more difficult to get an article published in a refereed journal. In actual fact the chief difference may be that it is likely to take somewhat longer to get an acceptance, or rejection, from a refereed journal since the editor must wait for a volunteer reader, who has other professional commitments, to read the article and offer comments.

In any case it is helpful to approach the editor in an intelligent manner. If the editor knows who you are and can see that your work is being presented thoughtfully, he is more likely to give it careful consideration. Professional journals will not agree to publish an article sight unseen unless they have commissioned it, and even in the case of commissioned articles they generally reserve the right not to publish something that does not meet their expectations. If you are considering a major piece of writing, however, it may not hurt to write an initial letter of inquiry to the editor describing yourself, what you propose to write on, the length of the article, your viewpoint, what it is that may be unusual about what you expect to say, and when you expect to have the article completed. By doing so you may be able to determine in advance whether or not your article, when finished, is likely to be appropriate for that journal. You may also obtain some advice about aspects of the subject that are of particular interest, or conversely of no interest, to that journal. In any case you may find that your article obtains a more favorable reception when it is received, provided it does what you said it would, than if it arrives at a journal totally unannounced. An expression of interest from a journal in response to a letter of inquiry should never be construed as a guarantee of publication, but it may save you considerable time and effort in the preparation of your work.

Submissions need not, and indeed should not, be accompanied by a full-scale resume, or by a multi-page letter repeating your professional history and the substance of your masterpiece and indicating why, in your opinion, it deserves to be published. A carefully prepared one-page cover letter that provides in a concise format information about your background, interests, and qualifications, and something about the article, is well worth the effort.

If you have already had work published in a particular journal, or if the editor knows of you and the quality of your written work, he or she may be more willing to consider future pieces. If you are interested in professional writing, therefore, it may help as a beginner to look for opportunities of a more limited and self-contained nature. Professional reviews, as short pieces with a defined focus, are, for example, an excellent starting point for the beginning professional writer. Not only do they provide practice in developing writing skills, but they help develop an entree with the journal editor. Watch for notices that reviewers are sought, or address a brief inquiry to the editor of a journal which you regularly read. Here again information about your background, interests, and qualifications may be helpful if presented concisely. It may also be helpful to include a sample review of a professional work that you have recently read which is carefully patterned after the format, length, and style of the particular journal. This is perhaps truest if the journal is not soliciting reviewers. Other writing opportunities—the preparation of material for local or state journals, or of news items, letters to the editor, and other brief items for national journals—both provide practice and help begin to identify you as a writer.

It is especially important to realize that the physical appearance of an article may well be a factor in its acceptance. Quality typing, with few or no visible corrections, done on an electric typewriter, is important. If you are not a good typist, it may even pay to hire a professional typist to prepare the final version of your manuscript. Proofread everything carefully. Careful preparation is particularly important because, in the case of most professional library journals, minimal editing is likely to be done by the journal's editorial staff. Some editing may be done, especially by the major national journals with a paid editorial staff, but in most cases if an article is accepted for publication it is likely to be published almost exactly as submitted.

It is a matter of common courtesy, as well as a standard practice, to submit an article to only one journal at a time and to give that editor a reasonable opportunity to respond. Patience is required. Response time as to whether or not your article has been accepted varies considerably, and as has been indicated is likely to be considerably longer for refereed journals, but you should allow at least a month, and perhaps longer, for a response. If you do not hear in what appears to be a reasonable length of time, as verified by the data provided in this guide, by all means inquire. Things do get lost in the mail, or in editorial offices, so be sure that you have kept a copy of your article. If you do not hear from an inquiry, you may wish to write again, after another reasonable period of time, indicating simply that since you have not heard you are assuming a lack of interest and are withdrawing your request that the editor consider your article for publication. That may, or may not, prompt a response but it certainly will provide you with other options to consider.

Not everything that you submit for publication will be accepted nor should you expect it to be. Be prepared for rejections, especially in your initial efforts, and be prepared especially for rejections that may not indicate very much about the reasons for the rejection.

What next? The simple approach is to try another journal, and another, and then another on the grounds—which some people, including many journal editors, maintain are true—that sooner or later almost anything you write, regardless of its quality, will be accepted and published by some journal. That may be true, but continued submission of the same product to different journals is not the most practical approach. Unless an editor indicates that he is rejecting your manuscript because it is outside the scope of his journal, or for some other reason having nothing to do with the content or quality of your work, it is best to assume that your ideas in that particular article may not be of any general interest, or that your writing needs improvement. The editor may, although it is more likely that he may not, indicate something about the reasons behind his rejection and may even make some suggestions, especially if the journal is refereed, about additions and changes that you should consider. It is best to let a rejected article sit for a while until you have overcome your disappointment or frustration at its rejection. Then read it again, seek more advice from your colleagues, and carefully consider if it deserves rewriting. In many cases it may not and it may be best to abandon the particular article or idea for the time being; but always retain a copy for possible future adaptation, incorporation into some other article, or use.

If, on reflection, you feel that the article does deserve rewriting, go back almost to the initial stage of preparation. It may take almost as long, except for the initial gathering of data and research and that may need to be updated or supplemented, to rewrite such an article as it did to write it initially. The article should be substantially rewritten and then compared with your original version to make sure that you can see a definite improvement before it is again submitted for publication. Unless the editor who originally rejected it has suggested a definite willingness to consider a revised and rewritten version, it is best to submit it to another journal at this time. Again in the rewriting process some thought should have been given to what that journal might be.

*Publication of an Article*

If, at last, your article is accepted for publication, you must again be patient and prepared for what often seems to be, and sometimes is, an interminable delay before it finally appears in print. The time lag between acceptance of an article and its publication varies widely from journal to journal as the data in the main section of this guide indicate; it may also vary with the importance, length, quality, and/or timeliness of an article. Depending on those and other factors, a six-month delay is not unusual and, in some cases, it may well be longer. At the time of acceptance one may ask the editor to anticipate when the article will be published; the information in this guide also gives some indication of what to expect from a specific journal. While it is unusual, sometimes an unreasonably long period of time passes and an article is not published and no explanation has been forthcoming. In such cases it does no harm to write a gentle letter of inquiry to the editor asking about the status of the article.

In most cases, as has been stressed, professional journals will do only minimal editing and what editing is done may well be done directly by the editor without consultation with the author. This is most true if the editing is for style, or if the article needs to be shortened for publication. If major changes are needed, it is more likely that they will be discussed with the author. Once the article has been typeset, proofreading may be handled entirely by the journal, or it may be passed on to the author. It is important to understand, if you are asked to do proofreading, that it is essential to comply fully with the time requirements (often asking for return within 24-48 hours of receipt) set by the publisher and to recognize that this is not the time to rewrite your article. Proofreading by the author is intended only to help catch grammatical and typographical errors, major omissions, and major errors of fact that may be more apparent in the final proofreading. In most cases extensive changes by the author at the proofreading stage may result in a delay in publication and in charges to the author for the costs involved in resetting of the article.

At least be thankful that most professional library journals, unlike many scientific journals and some information science journals, have not adopted the practice of asking an author or institution, once an article has been accepted for publication, to pay a charge of so much per page to partially subsidize the costs of publication. On the other hand you should realize, if you do encounter this situation, that this is an accepted professional practice not to be confused with vanity publishing in the monographic field. You may also encounter journals that provide for early publication, or the publication of articles that exceed their normal page limitations, on payment of part of the costs of publication. Again such a practice is acceptable. It provides a publisher, who is normally dependent upon a combination of advertising income and subscription income, some flexibility in meeting special conditions not planned for in the journal's budget.

On the other hand, you should not expect to get rich as a professional writer. For the most part professional writing in library and information science journals is on a no charge/no payment basis. A few of the major professional journals may pay modest honorariums for an article but most pay nothing at all.

Under the new copyright law in the absence of an express transfer of rights, the owner of the copyright in a collective publication, such as a journal, is presumed to have acquired only the privilege of publishing that contribution as part of that collective work, or as a part of revisions or continuations of it. Unless the journal asks for a transfer of rights, control of all republication rights remains with the author. For a variety of reasons—including the elimination of the need to keep track of the whereabouts of a number of authors over a long period of time, and of the need for those who may later wish to reprint an article to track down an author—most library and information science journals, like many other journals, routinely send authors a form asking that all republication rights, except for any use or republication by the original author, be transferred to the journal. Unless for some reason you feel a strong need to retain strict control over republication rights, it is probably best to comply with the requirements of a particular journal in this regard. You should be prepared, if you wish to suggest a policy other than that normally followed by the journal, for the journal to decline to publish your article on those grounds. Since anthologies are relatively common nowadays, and since a small fee ($25-$50 plus a copy of the book) may be paid for the rights to use material in an anthology, it may be worthwhile trying to retain some control over those rights if possible. At least it is helpful to be clear what the disposition of any fees for republication rights will be, although most frequently journals tend to pass those fees along to the initial author in any case.

Most journals will offer you a limited number of copies of the issue in which your article finally appears, or a limited number of reprints, free of charge; and some may offer to sell you additional reprints for a nominal charge. Unless you are certain that you have written a major piece that will generate numerous requests for copies, teach a class in which you plan to use the article, or have an inordinately large number of friends and relatives, it is a waste of money to invest in any sizeable number of reprints for they are most likely only to sit in a closet gathering dust.

*Conclusion*

At last your article has been published. What next? Don't expect any overwhelming response to your masterpiece no matter how brilliant you think it is. Others may read it and think about it, but only the most controversial, outrageous, provocative, or unusual article is likely to evoke any written response. An article which generates one or two personal letters to the author and a few letters to the editor is a major success.

After all, money and fame weren't your primary objectives in writing the article in the first place. If you have written and had published an article that you feel has provided useful information, has helped clarify your own ideas, has contributed to your own professional growth and development, and has made a contribution—no matter how slight—to librarianship, then you should be well content. Until, that is, you decide it is time to embark on the whole process again. In writing, as in other fields, nothing succeeds like success. Once you have had your first major article published, the next one is that much easier to do. In librarianship, as in other fields, most persons are not prolific authors. Don't feel that it is necessary to write frequently. The best writing comes when you have an idea or a subject about which you have something to say, in which you are keenly interested, and about which you can find a means of expressing your thoughts effectively.

Norman D. Stevens

## SELECTED BIBLIOGRAPHY

There are a substantial number of articles on writing for publication in the library press and an even larger number on the state of the library press and our professional literature. Those articles are useful to the prospective author because: (1) they offer advice or information about the practice of writing for publication; (2) they attempt to place the library press in perspective; or (3) they provide comment and interpretation about particular journals. Professional writing is a highly personal matter, especially in terms of approach and style, and we would urge prospective authors to read what others have to say. Although most of the articles on the state of the library press deplore the quality of the material that is published, it is useful to read such articles to gain some perspective on the situation. Such articles may also contain valuable comments on what to do, or more often what not to do, in preparing an article for publication. Finally, while the main body of this guide provides objective information about particular journals, the evaluative, and more subjective, comments about particular journals contained in some of the articles should also be of interest to the prospective author. Often the three kinds of articles described are not separate and distinct and there is considerable overlap. For purposes of convenience, however, we have attempted to designate the main theme of an article by placing a (1), (2), or (3) at the end of the citation to correspond with the categories as numbered above.

Beals, Ralph "Implications in Communications Research for the Public Library" in Douglas Waples, ed. *Print, Radio, and Film in a Democracy* Chicago, University of Chicago Press, 1942. p. 159-81. (2)

Becker, Philip G. "How to Write Effectively for a Library Periodical" *Wilson Library Bulletin* 31:539, 559, 1957. Reprinted in: Norman D. Stevens *Library Humor* Metuchen, NJ, Scarecrow Press, 1971. p. 145-7. (1)

Blake, Fay M. "A Look at Library Literature" *Wilson Library Bulletin* 35:715, 720, 1961. (1)

Bloomfield, Masse "A Quantitative Study of the Publishing Characteristics of Librarians" *Drexel Library Quarterly* 15:24-49, 1979 (July). (1)

## Selected Bibliography

Bloomfield, Masse "The Writing Habits of Librarians" *College & Research Libraries* 27:109-19, 1966. (1)

Bobinski, George, ed. "The Literature of Librarianship and Information Science" (Part I & II) *Drexel Library Quarterly* Volume 15, Numbers 1 and 3; January and July 1979. (1, 2, & 3)

Carnovsky, Leon "Standards for Library Periodicals" *Library Journal* 80:264-9, 1955. (2)

Collier, Bonnie "The Library Journals: Putting Things in Order" *Change* 6:59-61, 1974 (May). (3)

Danky, James P., and Fox, Michael "Alternative Periodicals" *Wilson Library Bulletin* 51:763-8, 1977. (3)

Danton, J. Periam "The Library Press" *Library Trends* 25:153-7, 1976. (2)

Davis, Jo-Ann, Boone, Roberta, and Hoadley, Irene Braden "Of Making Many Books: A Library Publication Program" *College & Research Libraries* 32:31-5, 1971. (1)

Edgar, Neal "Periodical Library Literature: A Centennial Assessment" *Serials Librarian* 2:341-50, 1978. (2 & 3)

Ferguson, Douglas "Disseminating Library and Information Science Research in the United States" *UNESCO Bulletin for Libraries* 29:319-38, 1975. (1)

Goldstein, Sam *CALL* Framingham, MA, Goldstein Associates. Volume 1, Number 1; 1972- . (1, 2, & 3)

Harreld, Jennie M. "Report on the Conference on Writing and Publishing for Librarians" *College & Research Libraries News* 36:177-9, 1975 (June). (1)

Horrocks, Norman "English Language Publishing in Librarianship Outside the United States" *Drexel Library Quarterly* 15:95-115, 1979 (July). (3)

Jones, Graham "This 'Incredible Stream of Garbage': The Library Journals, 1876-1975 *Indexer* 10:9-14, 1976 (April). Reprinted in: Bill Katz *Library Lit. 7—The Best of 1976* Metuchen, NJ, Scarecrow Press, 1977. p. 268-78. (2 & 3)

Lee, Joel, ed. "Library Periodicals in Review" *Serials Review* 5:7-39, 1979 (July/September). (3)

Lock, R. Northwood "Professional Literature: An Appreciation" in R. Northwood Lock, ed. *Manual of Library Economy* London, C. Bingley; Hamden, CT, Linnet Books, 1977. p. 429-34. (2 & 3)

Melin, Nancy Jean "The Specialization of Library Periodical Literature: Its Development and Status" *Drexel Library Quarterly* 15:25-51, 1979 (January). (3)

Moon, Eric "Dullness and Duplication" *Library Journal* 86:2760, 1961. Reprinted in: Eric Moon and Karl Nyren, ed. *Library Issues: The Sixties* New York, Bowker, 1970. p. 227-8. (2)

Moon, Eric "The Library Press" *Library Journal* 94:4104-9, 1969. Reprinted in: Bill Katz and Joel J. Schwartz *Library Lit. — The Best of 1970* Metuchen, NJ, Scarecrow Press, 1971. p. 10-25. (1)

Nelson, Jane L. "Academic Library Publications Committee: Twelve Years Later" *College & Research Libraries* 38:317-20, 1977. (1)

O'Connor, Daniel, and Van Orden, Phyllis "Getting Into Print" *College & Research Libraries* 39:389-96, 1978. (1)

Olive, Betsy Ann "Library Science — So What?; or, If Dewey Did It, You Can Too" *North Carolina Libraries* 13:101-3, 1955. Reprinted in: Norman D. Stevens *Library Humor* Metuchen, NJ, Scarecrow Press, 1971. p. 150-3. (1)

Olsgaard, John N., and Olsgaard, Jane Kinch "Authorship in Five Library Periodicals" *College & Research Libraries* 41:49-53, 1980. (1)

Palmer, Joseph W. "Non-Print Media About Librarianship and Information Science" *Drexel Library Quarterly* 15:52-76, 1979 (January). (3)

Rayman, Ronald, and Goudy, Frank William "Research and Publication Requirements in University Libraries" *College & Research Libraries* 41:43-8, 1980. (1)

Rayward, W. Boyd "Publishing Library Research" *College & Research Libraries* 41:210-9, 1980. (1)

Richardson, John V. "Readability and Readership of Journals in Library Science" *The Journal of Academic Librarianship* 3:20-2, 1977. (3)

Schuman, Patricia Glass, and Pedolsky, Andrea "Publishers of Library Science Books and Monographs" *Drexel Library Quarterly* 15:77-98, 1979 (January). (3)

Seaton, Janet "Readability Tests for UK Professional Journals" *Journal of Librarianship* 7:69-83, 1975. (3)

Shields, Gerald R. "The Library Press: National and State Magazines" *Drexel Library Quarterly* 15:3-24, 1979 (January). (3)

Stueart, Robert D. "Writing the Journal Article" *College & Research Libraries* 37:153-7, 1976. (1)

Stevens, Norman D., ed. *Essays from the New England Academic Librarians' Writing Seminar* Metuchen, NJ, Scarecrow Press, 1980.

Stevens, Norman D. "Writing for Publication" *Collection Management* 3:21-9, 1979. (1)

Shores, Louis "Press Proliferation: A Word for More" *RQ* 11:297-9, 1972. (1)

Taylor, Kenneth *Subjects of Articles Sought by Editors of Library and Information Science Periodicals* Villanova, PA, Villanova University Graduate Department of Library Science, 1979. (3)

Tegler, Patricia "Indexes and Abstracts of Library and Information Science" *Drexel Library Quarterly* 15:2-23, 1979 (July). (3)

Thompson, Donald E. "The Sad State of Library Literature" *ALA Bulletin* 55:642-4, 1961. (2)

Wasserman, Paul "The Influence of Education and Library Literature" in his *The New Librarianship: A Challenge for Change* New York, Bowker, 1972. p. 129-65. (3)

Watson, Paula DeSimone "Publication Activity Among Academic Librarians" *College & Research Libraries* 39:389-96, 1978. (1)

Werkley, Caroline E. "Not Everyone Likes Dragons" *Library Jounral* 94:4110-1, 1969. (1)

West, Celeste "Stop! The Print Is Killing Me!" *Synergy* 33:2-5, 1971 (Summer). (2)

## ABBREVIATIONS USED
### Abstracting and Indexing Services

| | |
|---|---|
| AB | Artbibliographies Modern |
| ABELL | Annual Bibliography of English Language & Literature |
| ABI | ABI/Inform |
| AC | American Cartographer |
| AES | Abstracts of English Studies |
| AHCI | Arts and Humanities Citation Index |
| AHL | America: History and Life |
| AI | Aslib Information |
| AL | Articles on American Literature |
| ARG | Abridged Readers' Guide to Periodical Literature |
| BAPI | British Alternative Press Index |
| BBF | Bulletin des Bibliothèques de France |
| BC | Bibliographia Cartographica |
| BEI | British Education Index |
| BHM | Bibliography of the History of Medicine |
| BKJ | Beiträge zur Kinder- und Jugendliteratur |
| BPI | Business Periodicals Index |
| BRD | Book Review Digest |
| BRI | Book Review Index |
| BS 101 | Bulletin Signalétique 101: Sciences de l'Information, Documentation |
| BiBI | Bibliographic Index |
| BioI | Biography Index |
| CA | Chemical Abstracts |
| CALL | Current Awareness = Library Literature |
| CARLD | Chicorel Abstracts to Reading and Learning Disabilities |
| CBI | Cumulative Book Index |
| CBRC | Current Book Review Citations |
| CC | Current Contents/Social & Behavioral Sciences |
| CCA | Computer and Control Abstracts |
| CIJE | Current Index to Journals in Education |
| CINL | Cumulative Index to Nursing Literature |
| CIS | Computer and Information Systems |
| CLA | Children's Literature Abstracts |
| CPI | Canadian Periodical Index |
| CPLI | Catholic Periodical & Literature Index |

| | |
|---|---|
| CR | Computing Reviews |
| CWHM | Current Work in the History of Medicine |
| Cerdic | Cerdic. Université des Sciences Humaines de Strasbourg |
| ChPI | Christian Periodical Index |
| DA | Documentation Abstracts |
| ECER | Exceptional Child Education Resources |
| EEA | Educational Administration Abstracts |
| EM | Excerpta Medica |
| EdI | Education Index |
| EnI | Engineering Index |
| FLI | Film Literature Index |
| FRAR | Fire Research Abstracts and Reviews |
| GAG | Geo Abstracts Part G |
| GPA | Guide to the Performing Arts |
| HA | Historical Abstracts |
| HLI | Hospital Literature Index |
| IB | Informationsdienst Bibliothekswesen |
| ICP | Index to Chinese Periodicals |
| IH | Information Hotline |
| IIFP | International Index to Film Periodicals |
| IIMII | International Index to Multi-Media Information |
| ILP | Index to Legal Periodicals |
| IM | Index Medicus |
| INSPEC | INSPEC Science Abstracts |
| IPARL | Index to Periodical Articles Related to Law |
| IRB | Indices De Revistas De Bibliotecologia |
| ISA | Information Science Abstracts |
| JCF | Journal of Canadian Fiction Annual Bibliography |
| LISA | Library & Information Science Abstracts |
| LL | Library Literature |
| LLBA | Language and Language Behavior Abstracts |
| MAG | Music Article Guide |
| MI | Magazine Index |
| MLA | MLA International Bibliography of Books and Articles on the Modern Languages and Literatures |
| MRD | Media Review Digest |
| MuI | Music Index |
| PA | Psychological Abstracts |
| PAIS | Public Affairs Information Service Bulletin |
| PH | Paedigogica Historica |
| PPI | Popular Periodical Index |
| QBCDP | Quarterly Bibliography of Computers and Data Processing |
| RBRI | Reference Book Review Index |

| | |
|---|---|
| RILM | RILM Abstracts of Music Literature |
| RSR | Reference Services Review |
| RZ | Referativnyĭ Zhurnal: Informatika |
| SA | Sociological Abstracts |
| SBPI | Southern Baptist Periodical Index |
| SCI | Science Citation Index |
| SSCI | Social Science Citation Index |
| SWRA | Social Work Research & Abstracts |

## ABBREVIATIONS USED
## Style Manuals

| | |
|---|---|
| APA | American Psychological Association *Publication Manual* (2d ed.) Washington, DC, 1974. 136 p. |
| Biology | Council of Biology Editors. Style Manual Committee *Council of Biology Editors Style Manual* (4th ed.) Arlington, VA, 1978. 265 p. |
| Burbidge | Burbidge, Peter George *Notes and References* Cambridge, Cambridge University Press, 1952. 19 p. |
| Chicago | University of Chicago Press *A Manual of Style* (12th ed.) Chicago, 1969. 545 p. |
| Collins | Collins, F. Howard *Authors and Printers Dictionary* (11th ed.) London, Oxford University Press, 1973. 474 p. |
| GPO | U.S. Government Printing Office *Style Manual* (Rev. ed.) Washington, DC, 1973. 548 p. |
| Hart's Rules | Hart, Horace *Rules for Compositors & Readers* (37th ed.) London, Oxford University Press, 1967. 141 p. |
| MLA | Modern Language Association *The MLA Style Sheet* (2nd ed.) New York, 1975. 48 p. |
| Skillin | Skillin, Marjorie E. *Words Into Type* (3rd ed.) Englewood Cliffs, NJ, Prentice Hall, 1974. 585 p. |
| Turabian | Turabian, Kate L. *A Manual of Term Papers, Theses, and Dissertations* (4th ed.) Chicago, University of Chicago Press, 1973. 216 p. |

**ALPHABETICAL LISTING OF JOURNALS**

**JOURNAL TITLE:** AJL Bulletin

**SUBSCRIPTION ADDRESS:** Mary G. Brand, 2842 Pine Tree Dr. #6, Miami Beach, FL. 33140

**PRICE:** $15
**CIRCULATION:** 650
**AFFILIATION:** Association of Jewish Libraries
**INDEXED/ABSTRACTED:** Not

**FREQUENCY:** Semiannual

**MANUSCRIPT ADDRESS:** Irene S. Levin, 48 Georgia St., Valley Stream, NY 11580

**EDITORIAL POLICY:** To publish materials and information to aid Judaica librarians in the performance of their duties

**AUDIENCE:** Librarians and others working in the field of Judaica
**PREFERRED TOPICS:** Judaic research, Bible study, bibliographies, resource materials, topics of Jewish interest

**INAPPROPRIATE TOPICS:** Original poetry

**FEATURES:** News, publications

**REVIEWS:** Yes

**STUDENT PAPERS:** Yes

**RESTRICTIONS:** None
**COVER LETTER:** Yes
**NUMBER OF COPIES:** 2
**STYLE:** None
**FORMAT:** Standard

**ABSTRACT:** No
**LENGTH:** 500-1,000
**INSTRUCTION FORM:** No

**ACKNOWLEDGED:** Yes
**REVIEW PROCESS:** Editorial board

**NOTIFICATION TIME:** 2 weeks

**CRITICISM:** No

**ACCEPTANCE RATE:** 95%
**REVISION:** Light
**EARLY PUBLICATION OPTION:** No
**COPYRIGHT POLICY:** Not copyrighted
**FEE:** None
**REPRINTS:** 5 copies of issue

**PUBLICATION TIME LAG:** Next issue
**PROOFS:** No
**PAGE CHARGES:** No

JOURNAL TITLE: APLA Bulletin

SUBSCRIPTION ADDRESS: Treasurer, APLA, c/o School of Library Service, Dalhousie University, Halifax, Nova Scotia B3H 4H8

PRICE: $10
CIRCULATION: 500
AFFILIATION: Atlantic Provinces Library Association
INDEXED/ABSTRACTED: CPI, LISA

FREQUENCY: 6 x a year

MANUSCRIPT ADDRESS: Peter Glenister, School of Library Service, Dalhousie University, Halifax, N.S. Canada B3H 4H8

EDITORIAL POLICY: Topics may deal with any area of knowledge related to information and its storage and dissemination in any format

AUDIENCE: APLA members

PREFERRED TOPICS: Development in fields essential to library operation, literacy, censorship, user reading and behavior habits

INAPPROPRIATE TOPICS: None given

FEATURES: Column on conservation

REVIEWS: No

STUDENT PAPERS: Yes

RESTRICTIONS: None
COVER LETTER: Yes
NUMBER OF COPIES: 1
STYLE: Turabian
FORMAT: Standard

ABSTRACT: No
LENGTH: 2,000-3,000
INSTRUCTION FORM: Yes

ACKNOWLEDGED: Yes
REVIEW PROCESS: Editor

NOTIFICATION TIME: 1 month

CRITICISM: No

ACCEPTANCE RATE: 90%
REVISION: Light
EARLY PUBLICATION OPTION: No
COPYRIGHT POLICY: Author and publisher
FEE: None
REPRINTS: 1; others may be purchased

PUBLICATION TIME LAG: 2-4 months
PROOFS: No
PAGE CHARGES: No

JOURNAL TITLE: American Archivist

SUBSCRIPTION ADDRESS: Society of American Archivists, 330 South Wells St., Suite 310, Chicago, IL 60606

PRICE: $25
CIRCULATION: 3,382
AFFILIATION: Society of American Archivists
INDEXED/ABSTRACTED: BRI, HA, LL

FREQUENCY: Quarterly

MANUSCRIPT ADDRESS: Virginia C. Purdy, The American Archivist, National Archives Building, Washington, DC 20408

EDITORIAL POLICY: Seeks to reflect the thinking of archivists about trends and major issues in archival philosophy and theory, and about the evolution of the archival profession in North America

AUDIENCE: Archivists

PREFERRED TOPICS: Analytical and critical expositions based on original research about subjects of broad interest, and accounts of innovative methods or techniques

INAPPROPRIATE TOPICS: How-we-do-it in our shop accounts

FEATURES: Technical notes (conservation of paper, tape, film); News of North American and other archives

REVIEWS: Yes                STUDENT PAPERS: Yes

RESTRICTIONS: None
COVER LETTER: Yes
NUMBER OF COPIES: 2
STYLE: Chicago
FORMAT: Standard

ABSTRACT: No
LENGTH: 5,000 or less
INSTRUCTION FORM: Yes

ACKNOWLEDGED: Yes            NOTIFICATION TIME: 2-3 months
REVIEW PROCESS: Editorial board and external reviewers

CRITICISM: Only if revision & resubmission are invited

ACCEPTANCE RATE: 20%
REVISION: Medium
EARLY PUBLICATION OPTION: No
COPYRIGHT POLICY: Publisher
FEE: None
REPRINTS: 10 tear sheets; others may be purchased

PUBLICATION TIME LAG: 6-12 months
PROOFS: Yes

PAGE CHARGES: No

**JOURNAL TITLE:** American Book Collector

**SUBSCRIPTION ADDRESS:** American Book Collector, 274 Madison Avenue, New York, NY 10016

**PRICE:** $16.50
**CIRCULATION:** 2,400
**AFFILIATION:** None
**INDEXED/ABSTRACTED:** AB, AES, BRI, MLA

**FREQUENCY:** 6 x a year

**MANUSCRIPT ADDRESS:** American Book Collector, 274 Madison Avenue, New York, NY 10016

**EDITORIAL POLICY:** Articles, reviews, interviews, columns, and news about book collecting written for collectors by other collectors, booksellers, and librarians

**AUDIENCE:** Book collectors

**PREFERRED TOPICS:** Book collecting, personal narratives of book collecting successes and failures

**INAPPROPRIATE TOPICS:** Not given

**FEATURES:** Not given

**REVIEWS:** Yes

**STUDENT PAPERS:** No

**RESTRICTIONS:** None
**COVER LETTER:** Yes
**NUMBER OF COPIES:** 2
**STYLE:** House stylesheet
**FORMAT:** Standard

**ABSTRACT:** No
**LENGTH:** 1,500-3,000
**INSTRUCTION FORM:** Yes

**ACKNOWLEDGED:** Yes
**REVIEW PROCESS:** Editorial board

**NOTIFICATION TIME:** 1-5 weeks

**CRITICISM:** No

**ACCEPTANCE RATE:** Most articles
**REVISION:** Light
**EARLY PUBLICATION OPTION:** No
**COPYRIGHT POLICY:** Publisher
**FEE:** Only by arrangement for certain solicited articles
**REPRINTS:** 5 copies of issue; others may be purchased

**PUBLICATION TIME LAG:** 2-4 months
**PROOFS:** No
**PAGE CHARGES:** No

JOURNAL TITLE: American Libraries

SUBSCRIPTION ADDRESS: Subscription Department, American Library Association, 50 E. Huron St., Chicago, IL 60611

PRICE: Through ALA membership  FREQUENCY: 11 x a year
CIRCULATION: 39,000
AFFILIATION: American Library Association
INDEXED/ABSTRACTED: EdI, ISA, LISA, LL, MI

MANUSCRIPT ADDRESS: Arthur Plotnik, American Libraries, American Library Association, 50 E. Huron St., Chicago, IL 60611

EDITORIAL POLICY: Primary objectives are communicating with the membership about the goals, activities, and business of the Association; providing news of developments in librarianship and advances in library service
AUDIENCE: Full membership of ALA
PREFERRED TOPICS: Research articles without academic trappings, commentaries, case studies, theoretical articles, book reviews, review articles, bibliographies, library information on developments of national significance
INAPPROPRIATE TOPICS: Off-the-cuff theories of why libraries "fail"; notes on minor meetings

FEATURES: Library life: pictorial view of activities with human interest pitch; On My Mind (800-1,000 word forum for strongly-held views); Mediatmosphere: AV features
REVIEWS: Professional books only  STUDENT PAPERS: Yes

RESTRICTIONS: None
COVER LETTER: Yes  ABSTRACT: No
NUMBER OF COPIES: 1  LENGTH: 2,000-2,500
STYLE: Chicago (flexible)  INSTRUCTION FORM: Yes
FORMAT: Standard

ACKNOWLEDGED: Yes (postcard)  NOTIFICATION TIME: 4-8 weeks
REVIEW PROCESS: At least three professional staff librarians/editors review appropriate submissions; external reviewer may be consulted
CRITICISM: No

ACCEPTANCE RATE: 10-20%  PUBLICATION TIME LAG: 1-6 months
REVISION: Medium to heavy  PROOFS: No
EARLY PUBLICATION OPTION: No  PAGE CHARGES: No
COPYRIGHT POLICY: Author, after 3 months from publication
FEE: $35-150
REPRINTS: 6 copies of issue; others may be purchased

**JOURNAL TITLE:** American Society for Information Science, Bulletin

**SUBSCRIPTION ADDRESS:** American Society for Information Science, 1010 16th St., N.W., Washington, DC 20036

**PRICE:** $27.50
**CIRCULATION:** 4,500
**AFFILIATION:** American Society for Information Science
**INDEXED/ABSTRACTED:** ABI, AI, CC, CIJE, ISA, LL, MI
**FREQUENCY:** 6 x a year

**MANUSCRIPT ADDRESS:** Bulletin, American Society for Information Science, 1010 16th St., N.W., Washington, DC 20036

**EDITORIAL POLICY:** To inform its readers of progress in information science, to interpret the meaning and discuss the implications of these advances, to describe information needs in society
**AUDIENCE:** ASIS members, information professionals
**PREFERRED TOPICS:** Commentaries, review articles, case studies

**INAPPROPRIATE TOPICS:** Book reviews

**FEATURES:** Reports of meetings and news

**REVIEWS:** No
**STUDENT PAPERS:** Yes

**RESTRICTIONS:** None
**COVER LETTER:** Yes
**NUMBER OF COPIES:** 1
**STYLE:** None
**FORMAT:** Standard
**ABSTRACT:** No
**LENGTH:** 900-1,800
**INSTRUCTION FORM:** No

**ACKNOWLEDGED:** Yes
**REVIEW PROCESS:** Editorial board
**NOTIFICATION TIME:** 1-2 months

**CRITICISM:** No

**ACCEPTANCE RATE:** 50%
**REVISION:** Light
**EARLY PUBLICATION OPTION:** No
**COPYRIGHT POLICY:** Publisher
**FEE:** None
**REPRINTS:** None; may be purchased if requested
**PUBLICATION TIME LAG:** 4 months
**PROOFS:** No
**PAGE CHARGES:** No

**JOURNAL TITLE:** American Society for Information Science. Journal

**SUBSCRIPTION ADDRESS:** Subscription Department, John Wiley & Sons, 605 Third Avenue, New York, NY 10016

**PRICE:** $50
**CIRCULATION:** 6,177
**AFFILIATION:** American Society for Information Science
**INDEXED/ABSTRACTED:** CA, CC, CR, EnI, ISA, LISA, LL, SCI, SSCI
**FREQUENCY:** 6 x a year

**MANUSCRIPT ADDRESS:** Charles T. Meadow, Graduate School of Library Science, Drexel University, Philadelphia, PA 19104

**EDITORIAL POLICY:** All aspects of information science; research findings; opinions; and practical applications of information systems or technology

**AUDIENCE:** Persons interested in information science research, system design, management, and information economics

**PREFERRED TOPICS:** Reports of original research, reports of significant new systems, opinion papers on any topic within scope

**INAPPROPRIATE TOPICS:** Poorly documented research, proposals for new systems without results

**FEATURES:** Book reviews, Perspectives (tutorial and editorial articles on a single subject)

**REVIEWS:** Yes, of books applicable to information science
**STUDENT PAPERS:** No

**RESTRICTIONS:** None
**COVER LETTER:** No
**NUMBER OF COPIES:** 3
**STYLE:** Biology
**FORMAT:** Standard
**ABSTRACT:** 200
**LENGTH:** 5,000
**INSTRUCTION FORM:** Yes

**ACKNOWLEDGED:** Yes
**REVIEW PROCESS:** External reviewers
**NOTIFICATION TIME:** 2-6 months

**CRITICISM:** Only to extent of providing reviewer's comments

**ACCEPTANCE RATE:** 80%
**REVISION:** Light
**EARLY PUBLICATION OPTION:** No
**COPYRIGHT POLICY:** Publisher
**FEE:** None
**REPRINTS:** None; may be purchased
**PUBLICATION TIME LAG:** 12 months
**PROOFS:** Yes
**PAGE CHARGES:** No

JOURNAL TITLE: The Amoxcalli Newsletter

SUBSCRIPTION ADDRESS: Amoxcalli, P.O. Box 2064, El Paso, TX 79951

PRICE: $5
CIRCULATION: 800
AFFILIATION: Reforma--El Paso Chapter
INDEXED/ABSTRACTED: Not

FREQUENCY: Quarterly

MANUSCRIPT ADDRESS: Amoxcalli, P.O. Box 2064, El Paso, TX 79951

EDITORIAL POLICY: An information source for librarians serving Spanish speaking people in all locales

AUDIENCE: Librarians, educators, students

PREFERRED TOPICS: Any aspect of library service to minorities, especially Hispanics

INAPPROPRIATE TOPICS: None given

FEATURES: None

REVIEWS: Yes

STUDENT PAPERS: No

RESTRICTIONS: None
COVER LETTER: No
NUMBER OF COPIES: 2
STYLE: None
FORMAT: Standard

ABSTRACT: No
LENGTH: 1,000
INSTRUCTION FORM: No

ACKNOWLEDGED: Yes
REVIEW PROCESS: Editorial board

NOTIFICATION TIME: 2-3 weeks

CRITICISM: Yes

ACCEPTANCE RATE: 90%
REVISION: Medium
EARLY PUBLICATION OPTION: No
COPYRIGHT POLICY: Publisher and author
FEE: None
REPRINTS: 5 copies of issue; additional copies if available

PUBLICATION TIME LAG: 3 months
PROOFS: No
PAGE CHARGES: No

**JOURNAL TITLE:** Annals of Library Science and Documentation

**SUBSCRIPTION ADDRESS:** INSDOC, Hillside Road, New Delhi, 110012 India

**PRICE:** $15
**CIRCULATION:** 500
**AFFILIATION:** Indian National Scientific Documentation Centre
**INDEXED/ABSTRACTED:** CA, IH, LISA, LL, RZ
**FREQUENCY:** Quarterly

**MANUSCRIPT ADDRESS:** B. Guha, INSDOC, Hillside Road, New Delhi, 110012 India

**EDITORIAL POLICY:** To publish original contributions in the field of library classification, cataloguing, bibliographic organization, documentation techniques, bibliographic standardization, reprographic methods, etc.

**AUDIENCE:** Librarians and information science workers

**PREFERRED TOPICS:** Reports of actual application of modern techniques, new innovations, etc.

**INAPPROPRIATE TOPICS:** Articles describing techniques in general

**FEATURES:** None

**REVIEWS:** Yes

**STUDENT PAPERS:** No

**RESTRICTIONS:** None
**COVER LETTER:** Yes
**NUMBER OF COPIES:** 2
**STYLE:** Not given
**FORMAT:** Standard
**ABSTRACT:** 300
**LENGTH:** No limit
**INSTRUCTION FORM:** No

**ACKNOWLEDGED:** Yes
**REVIEW PROCESS:** Editorial board
**NOTIFICATION TIME:** 1 month

**CRITICISM:** No

**ACCEPTANCE RATE:** 80%
**REVISION:** Light
**EARLY PUBLICATION OPTION:** No
**COPYRIGHT POLICY:** Publisher
**FEE:** None
**REPRINTS:** 20; additional copies not encouraged
**PUBLICATION TIME LAG:** up to 1 year
**PROOFS:** No
**PAGE CHARGES:** No

JOURNAL TITLE: Archivaria

SUBSCRIPTION ADDRESS: Archivaria, Room 349, Public Archives of Canada, 395 Wellington St., Ottawa K1A ON 3, Canada

PRICE: $12
CIRCULATION: 850
AFFILIATION: Association of Canadian Archivists
INDEXED/ABSTRACTED: Not

FREQUENCY: Semiannual

MANUSCRIPT ADDRESS: Archivaria, Room 349, Public Archives of Canada, 395 Wellington St., Ottawa K1A ON3, Canada

EDITORIAL POLICY: Articles and reviews which are of enduring value concerning archives and archivists

AUDIENCE: Archivists, researchers

PREFERRED TOPICS: Anything related to use or control of archival resources in any medium

INAPPROPRIATE TOPICS: Not given

FEATURES: Theme issues (labor, photography, freedom of information, medicine, conservation)

REVIEWS: Yes

STUDENT PAPERS: No

RESTRICTIONS: None
COVER LETTER: Yes
NUMBER OF COPIES: 2
STYLE: None
FORMAT: Standard

ABSTRACT: 300
LENGTH: 10,000
INSTRUCTION FORM: Yes

ACKNOWLEDGED: Yes
REVIEW PROCESS: External reviewers

NOTIFICATION TIME: 1 month

CRITICISM: Usually

ACCEPTANCE RATE: 10%
REVISION: Heavy
EARLY PUBLICATION OPTION: No
COPYRIGHT POLICY: Author and publisher
FEE: None
REPRINTS: 10; others may be purchased

PUBLICATION TIME LAG: 5 months
PROOFS: No

PAGE CHARGES: No

JOURNAL TITLE: Archives

SUBSCRIPTION ADDRESS: British Records Association, Masters Court, The Charterhouse, Charterhouse Square, London EC1M 6AU England

PRICE: $17
CIRCULATION: 1,300
AFFILIATION: British Records Association
INDEXED/ABSTRACTED: LISA, LL

FREQUENCY: Semiannual

MANUSCRIPT ADDRESS: A. S. Cook, Journal of the British Records Association, India Office Library and Records, 197 Blackfriars Road, London SE1 8NG, England

EDITORIAL POLICY: Academic articles on archival history, documentary history, archives

AUDIENCE: Historians, archivists, owners of historical manuscripts, conservators, librarians

PREFERRED TOPICS: All aspects of the ownership, custody, preservation, study and publication of archives

INAPPROPRIATE TOPICS: Economic and social history

FEATURES: Local Archives in Great Britain

REVIEWS: Yes
STUDENT PAPERS: No

RESTRICTIONS: None
COVER LETTER: Yes
NUMBER OF COPIES: 1
STYLE: See journal
FORMAT: Standard

ABSTRACT: No
LENGTH: 8,000
INSTRUCTION FORM: No

ACKNOWLEDGED: Yes
REVIEW PROCESS: Editorial board

NOTIFICATION TIME: 3-8 weeks

CRITICISM: No

ACCEPTANCE RATE: Not given
REVISION: Light
EARLY PUBLICATION OPTION: No
COPYRIGHT POLICY: Author and publisher
FEE: None
REPRINTS: 6; others may be purchased

PUBLICATION TIME LAG: 6-12 months
PROOFS: Yes
PAGE CHARGES: No

**JOURNAL TITLE:** Aslib Proceedings

**SUBSCRIPTION ADDRESS:** Subscriptions, Aslib, 3 Belgrave Square, London SW1X 8PL, England

**PRICE:** 38 pounds
**CIRCULATION:** 3,500
**AFFILIATION:** Aslib
**INDEXED/ABSTRACTED:** LISA, LL
**FREQUENCY:** Monthly

**MANUSCRIPT ADDRESS:** Kathleen Gray, Aslib Proceedings, 3 Belgrave Square, London SW1X 8PL, England

**EDITORIAL POLICY:** Carries papers given at Aslib meetings & conferences, and contributed papers of interest to practising professionals

**AUDIENCE:** Practising special librarians & information scientists

**PREFERRED TOPICS:** Innovations in information management techniques, applications of existing information products and services, and case studies of information units and special libraries

**INAPPROPRIATE TOPICS:** Book reviews

**FEATURES:** Library management series

**REVIEWS:** No
**STUDENT PAPERS:** No

**RESTRICTIONS:** None
**COVER LETTER:** Yes
**NUMBER OF COPIES:** 1
**STYLE:** Hart's Rules
**FORMAT:** Standard; reproducible figures
**ABSTRACT:** 200
**LENGTH:** 1,000-3,000
**INSTRUCTION FORM:** Yes

**ACKNOWLEDGED:** Yes
**REVIEW PROCESS:** Editorial board
**NOTIFICATION TIME:** 1-2 weeks

**CRITICISM:** No

**ACCEPTANCE RATE:** 50%
**REVISION:** Light
**EARLY PUBLICATION OPTION:** No
**COPYRIGHT POLICY:** Author and publisher
**FEE:** None
**REPRINTS:** 25; others may be purchased
**PUBLICATION TIME LAG:** 4-6 months
**PROOFS:** Yes
**PAGE CHARGES:** No

**JOURNAL TITLE:** Association for Recorded Sound Collections. Journal

**SUBSCRIPTION ADDRESS:** Executive Secretary, ARSC, P.O. Box 1643, Manassas, VA 22110

**PRICE:** $10
**FREQUENCY:** Quarterly
**CIRCULATION:** 750
**AFFILIATION:** Association for Recorded Sound Collections
**INDEXED/ABSTRACTED:** MAG, MuI

**MANUSCRIPT ADDRESS:** Executive Secretary, ARSC, P.O. Box 1643, Manassas, VA 22110

**EDITORIAL POLICY:** To publish articles, discographies, bibliographies, and reviews of scholarly interest in the field of sound recordings and sound archives

**AUDIENCE:** Anyone interested in sound recordings and sound archives

**PREFERRED TOPICS:** Sound recordings and sound archives

**INAPPROPRIATE TOPICS:** Book reviews

**FEATURES:** Bibliography of discographies

**REVIEWS:** Yes (of recordings of historical interest)
**STUDENT PAPERS:** Yes

**RESTRICTIONS:** None
**COVER LETTER:** Yes
**NUMBER OF COPIES:** 2
**STYLE:** MLA
**FORMAT:** Standard
**ABSTRACT:** No
**LENGTH:** 2,500 plus
**INSTRUCTION FORM:** Yes

**ACKNOWLEDGED:** Yes
**REVIEW PROCESS:** External reviewers
**NOTIFICATION TIME:** 1 month

**CRITICISM:** Yes

**ACCEPTANCE RATE:** 95%
**REVISION:** Light
**EARLY PUBLICATION OPTION:** No
**COPYRIGHT POLICY:** Publisher
**FEE:** None
**REPRINTS:** 10
**PUBLICATION TIME LAG:** 1 year
**PROOFS:** Not unless requested
**PAGE CHARGES:** No

**JOURNAL TITLE:** Behavioral & Social Sciences Librarian

**SUBSCRIPTION ADDRESS:** Haworth Press, 28 East 22 Street, New York, NY 10010

**PRICE:** $25
**CIRCULATION:** 500
**AFFILIATION:** None
**INDEXED/ABSTRACTED:** CALL, EM, ISA, LISA, LL, SA, SWRA

**FREQUENCY:** Quarterly

**MANUSCRIPT ADDRESS:** Lucile Stark, Behavioral & Social Services Librarian, Staff Library, Western Psychiatric Institute, 3881 O'Hara Street, Pittsburgh, PA 15261

**EDITORIAL POLICY:** Scholarly periodical devoted to all areas of librarianship pertaining to the behavioral and social sciences

**AUDIENCE:** Behavioral and social science librarians, and faculty and scholars in those fields

**PREFERRED TOPICS:** Full-length review and research articles; comparative and/or critical reviews of journals; substantial reviews of major reference materials

**INAPPROPRIATE TOPICS:** Poorly written "how we did it" articles; reprints

**FEATURES:** Subject journal review in . . . (specialized discipline), Online articles relevant to behavioral and social science disciplines

**REVIEWS:** Yes        **STUDENT PAPERS:** Yes

**RESTRICTIONS:** None
**COVER LETTER:** Yes
**NUMBER OF COPIES:** 3
**STYLE:** Chicago
**FORMAT:** Standard

**ABSTRACT:** 100
**LENGTH:** Varies
**INSTRUCTION FORM:** Yes

**ACKNOWLEDGED:** Yes        **NOTIFICATION TIME:** 4-8 weeks
**REVIEW PROCESS:** Editor, editorial board, and external reviewers

**CRITICISM:** Yes

**ACCEPTANCE RATE:** 60%
**REVISION:** Medium
**EARLY PUBLICATION OPTION:** Yes
**COPYRIGHT POLICY:** Publisher
**FEE:** None
**REPRINTS:** 10

**PUBLICATION TIME LAG:** 6 months
**PROOFS:** Yes
**PAGE CHARGES:** No

JOURNAL TITLE: Brio

SUBSCRIPTION ADDRESS: Miss Ruth Davies, Cambridge College of Arts & Technology, Collier Rd., Cambridge, England

PRICE: $10
CIRCULATION: 500
AFFILIATION: International Association of Music Libraries
INDEXED/ABSTRACTED: RILM
FREQUENCY: Biannual

MANUSCRIPT ADDRESS: International Assn. of Music Libraries, United Kingdom Branch, c/o Alan Sopher, Central Music Lib., 160 Buckingham Palace Rd., London SW1W 9UD

EDITORIAL POLICY: Reports of conferences of the association, articles of interest to British music librarians, reviews of musico-bibliographical works, and other standard musical reference works

AUDIENCE: Music librarians

PREFERRED TOPICS: Music bibliography, or music librarianship

INAPPROPRIATE TOPICS: Not given

FEATURES: Not given

REVIEWS: Yes
STUDENT PAPERS: No

RESTRICTIONS: None
COVER LETTER: Yes
NUMBER OF COPIES: 1
STYLE: Not given
FORMAT: Not given
ABSTRACT: No
LENGTH: Varies
INSTRUCTION FORM: No

ACKNOWLEDGED: Yes
REVIEW PROCESS: Editorial board
NOTIFICATION TIME: 2-4 weeks

CRITICISM: Yes

ACCEPTANCE RATE: Articles requested
REVISION: Light
EARLY PUBLICATION OPTION: Not given
COPYRIGHT POLICY: Author and publisher
FEE: None
REPRINTS: Flexible
PUBLICATION TIME LAG: 6 months
PROOFS: No
PAGE CHARGES: Not given

**JOURNAL TITLE:** Bulletin of Bibliography

**SUBSCRIPTION ADDRESS:** Bulletin of Bibliography, Publications Division, F.W. Faxon Co., 15 Southwest Park, Westwood, MA 02090

**PRICE:** $18
**CIRCULATION:** 1,200
**AFFILIATION:** None
**INDEXED/ABSTRACTED:** AL, ABELL, BibI, BioI, CALL

**FREQUENCY:** Quarterly

**MANUSCRIPT ADDRESS:** Sandra Conrad, F.W. Faxon Co., 15 Southwest Park, Westwood, MA 02090

**EDITORIAL POLICY:** Publishes bibliographies on a wide range of topics in the humanities and social sciences

**AUDIENCE:** Not given

**PREFERRED TOPICS:** Bibliographies in the social sciences and humanities

**INAPPROPRIATE TOPICS:** Anything other than bibliographies

**FEATURES:** Not given

**REVIEWS:** No

**STUDENT PAPERS:** No

**RESTRICTIONS:** None
**COVER LETTER:** Required
**NUMBER OF COPIES:** 2
**STYLE:** MLA
**FORMAT:** Standard

**ABSTRACT:** No
**LENGTH:** 50 pages
**INSTRUCTION FORM:** Yes

**ACKNOWLEDGED:** Yes
**REVIEW PROCESS:** External reviewer

**NOTIFICATION TIME:** 2-3 months

**CRITICISM:** Yes

**ACCEPTANCE RATE:** Not given
**REVISION:** Medium
**EARLY PUBLICATION OPTION:** No
**COPYRIGHT POLICY:** Publisher
**FEE:** None
**REPRINTS:** 10

**PUBLICATION TIME LAG:** 12-18 months
**PROOFS:** Yes

**PAGE CHARGES:** No

**JOURNAL TITLE:** COLT Newsletter

**SUBSCRIPTION ADDRESS:** Richard L. Taylor, COLT Newsletter, Wright College LRC, 3400 N. Austin Ave., Chicago, IL 60634

**PRICE:** $10
**CIRCULATION:** 450
**AFFILIATION:** Council on Library/Media Technical Assistants
**INDEXED/ABSTRACTED:** Not

**FREQUENCY:** Monthly

**MANUSCRIPT ADDRESS:** Richard L. Taylor, COLT Newsletter, Wright College LRC, 3400 N. Austin Ave., Chicago, IL 60634

**EDITORIAL POLICY:** Carries news and articles related to training, placement and continuing education of library/media technical assistants

**AUDIENCE:** COLT members, LTA libraries and programs

**PREFERRED TOPICS:** Those concerned with the welfare and development of library technicians

**INAPPROPRIATE TOPICS:** Not given

**FEATURES:** Not given

**REVIEWS:** Yes

**STUDENT PAPERS:** Yes

**RESTRICTIONS:** None
**COVER LETTER:** Yes
**NUMBER OF COPIES:** 1
**STYLE:** Turabian
**FORMAT:** Standard

**ABSTRACT:** No
**LENGTH:** 1,000-2,000
**INSTRUCTION FORM:** Yes

**ACKNOWLEDGED:** Yes
**REVIEW PROCESS:** Editorial board

**NOTIFICATION TIME:** 1 montj

**CRITICISM:** No

**ACCEPTANCE RATE:** 70%
**REVISION:** Medium
**EARLY PUBLICATION OPTION:** No
**COPYRIGHT POLICY:** Not copyrighted
**FEE:** None
**REPRINTS:** 3

**PUBLICATION TIME LAG:** 2-3 months
**PROOFS:** If requested

**PAGE CHARGES:** No

JOURNAL TITLE: Canadian Children's Literature

SUBSCRIPTION ADDRESS: Canadian Children's Literature, Box 335, Guelph, Ontario N1H 6K5 Canada

PRICE: $12
CIRCULATION: Not given
AFFILIATION: None
INDEXED/ABSTRACTED: CLA, CPI, JCF

FREQUENCY: Quarterly

MANUSCRIPT ADDRESS: John R. Sorfleet, CC Press, P.O. Box 335, Guelph, Ontario N1H 6K5 Canada

EDITORIAL POLICY: Devoted to the literary analysis, criticism and review of books written for Canadian children.

AUDIENCE: Librarians, teachers, professors of children's literature, parents
PREFERRED TOPICS: Articles on any aspect of Canadian children's literature, either current or early literature

INAPPROPRIATE TOPICS: Creative material

FEATURES: Scholarly articles and interviews with Canadian writers or illustrators

REVIEWS: Yes
STUDENT PAPERS: Yes

RESTRICTIONS: None
COVER LETTER: Yes
NUMBER OF COPIES: 1
STYLE: House
FORMAT: Not given
ABSTRACT: No
LENGTH: Not given
INSTRUCTION FORM: Not given

ACKNOWLEDGED: Yes
REVIEW PROCESS: Editorial board and external reviewers
NOTIFICATION TIME: 1-6 months

CRITICISM: No

ACCEPTANCE RATE: Not given
REVISION: Light
EARLY PUBLICATION OPTION: No
COPYRIGHT POLICY: Publisher
FEE: $25-$50
REPRINTS: None
PUBLICATION TIME LAG: 1 year
PROOFS: No
PAGE CHARGES: No

**JOURNAL TITLE:** Canadian Journal of Information Science

**SUBSCRIPTION ADDRESS:** CAJS/ACSI Secretariat, The University of Calgary, The Library, Calgary, Alberta, Canada

**PRICE:** $10
**CIRCULATION:** 1,000
**AFFILIATION:** Canadian Association for Information Science
**INDEXED/ABSTRACTED:** Not given
**FREQUENCY:** Annual

**MANUSCRIPT ADDRESS:** Frank T. Dolan, Canadian Journal of Information Science, Box 158A, Terminal A, Ottawa, K1N 8V2, Canada

**EDITORIAL POLICY:** Describes Canadian work and problems in information science

**AUDIENCE:** Information science community in Canada and, secondarily, abroad

**PREFERRED TOPICS:** Research papers, theoretical analysis, empirical studies, policy analyses

**INAPPROPRIATE TOPICS:** The how-we-do-it-good-in-our-library type

**FEATURES:** Primers on "new" facets of information science

**REVIEWS:** Yes
**STUDENT PAPERS:** Yes

**RESTRICTIONS:** None
**COVER LETTER:** No
**NUMBER OF COPIES:** 3
**STYLE:** House
**FORMAT:** Standard
**ABSTRACT:** 50-100
**LENGTH:** 4,000
**INSTRUCTION FORM:** Yes

**ACKNOWLEDGED:** Yes
**REVIEW PROCESS:** External reviewers
**NOTIFICATION TIME:** Not given

**CRITICISM:** If requested

**ACCEPTANCE RATE:** 50%
**REVISION:** Light
**EARLY PUBLICATION OPTION:** No
**COPYRIGHT POLICY:** Publisher
**FEE:** None
**REPRINTS:** None; available at cost
**PUBLICATION TIME LAG:** 3 months
**PROOFS:** No
**PAGE CHARGES:** No

**JOURNAL TITLE:** Canadian Library Journal

**SUBSCRIPTION ADDRESS:** Subscriptions Manager, Canadian Library Association, 151 Sparks St., Ottawa, Ontario, K1P 5E3, Canada

**PRICE:** $17
**CIRCULATION:** 6,200
**AFFILIATION:** Canadian Library Association
**INDEXED/ABSTRACTED:** CPI, IIMII, LISA, LL
**FREQUENCY:** Bimonthly

**MANUSCRIPT ADDRESS:** Editor, Canadian Library Journal, Canadian Library Association, 151 Sparks St., Ottawa, Ontario, K1P 5E3, Canada

**EDITORIAL POLICY:** A professional journal that provides a forum for the discussion, analysis and evaluation of issues in librarianship.

**AUDIENCE:** Librarians, trustees and students

**PREFERRED TOPICS:** All topics acceptable

**INAPPROPRIATE TOPICS:** Unsolicited book reviews

**FEATURES:** Not given

**REVIEWS:** Only those solicited from members
**STUDENT PAPERS:** Yes

**RESTRICTIONS:** None
**COVER LETTER:** No
**NUMBER OF COPIES:** 2
**STYLE:** House
**FORMAT:** Standard
**ABSTRACT:** No
**LENGTH:** 2,500-7,500
**INSTRUCTION FORM:** Yes

**ACKNOWLEDGED:** Yes
**REVIEW PROCESS:** Editorial board
**NOTIFICATION TIME:** 2-4 months

**CRITICISM:** If time available

**ACCEPTANCE RATE:** 75%
**REVISION:** Medium
**EARLY PUBLICATION OPTION:** No
**COPYRIGHT POLICY:** Author
**FEE:** None
**REPRINTS:** 3; more if available
**PUBLICATION TIME LAG:** 2-4 months
**PROOFS:** If possible
**PAGE CHARGES:** No

JOURNAL TITLE: Cataloging & Classification Quarterly

SUBSCRIPTION ADDRESS: Haworth Press, 28 East 22 Street, New York, NY 10010

PRICE: $35
CIRCULATION: (New journal)
AFFILIATION: None
INDEXED/ABSTRACTED: Not yet

FREQUENCY: Quarterly

MANUSCRIPT ADDRESS: C. Donald Cook, Faculty of Library Science, University of Toronto, 140 St. George Street, Toronto, Ontario M5S 1A1, Canada

EDITORIAL POLICY: An international forum for information and discussion in the field of bibliographic organization

AUDIENCE: Catalogers and classification specialists; technical services professionals

PREFERRED TOPICS: Research and review articles; descriptions of new programs and technology, and material related to improving methods of bibliographic control for the future

INAPPROPRIATE TOPICS: Not given

FEATURES: Not given

REVIEWS: Not given

STUDENT PAPERS: Yes

RESTRICTIONS: None
COVER LETTER: Yes
NUMBER OF COPIES: 3
STYLE: Chicago
FORMAT: Standard

ABSTRACT: Not given
LENGTH: Not given
INSTRUCTION FORM: Yes

ACKNOWLEDGED: Yes
REVIEW PROCESS: Editorial board and external reviewers

NOTIFICATION TIME: Varies

CRITICISM: No

ACCEPTANCE RATE: To be determined
REVISION: Medium
EARLY PUBLICATION OPTION: Yes
COPYRIGHT POLICY: Publisher
FEE: None
REPRINTS: 10

PUBLICATION TIME LAG: Varies
PROOFS: Yes
PAGE CHARGES: No

JOURNAL TITLE: Catalogue & Index

SUBSCRIPTION ADDRESS: Catalogue & Index, C. J. Koster, 18 Apple Grove, Enfield, Middlesex, EN 1 3DD England

PRICE: $11
CIRCULATION: 3,500
FREQUENCY: Quarterly
AFFILIATION: Library Association. Cataloguing & Indexing Group
INDEXED/ABSTRACTED: Not given

MANUSCRIPT ADDRESS: Russell Sweeney, Catalogue & Index, Library Association, Cataloguing and Indexing Group, Department of Librarianship, Leeds Polytechnic, Leeds BS1 2SY, England

EDITORIAL POLICY: To encourage discussion of topics regarded as significant within the fields of bibliographic control, description & information retrieval.

AUDIENCE: Indexers, cataloguers, classifiers

PREFERRED TOPICS: Bibliographic control and information retrieval

INAPPROPRIATE TOPICS: Critical letters

FEATURES: Not given

REVIEWS: By invitation only       STUDENT PAPERS: No

RESTRICTIONS: None
COVER LETTER: Yes
NUMBER OF COPIES: 2
STYLE: House
FORMAT: Line length of 54 characters
ABSTRACT: No
LENGTH: 2,500
INSTRUCTION FORM: Yes

ACKNOWLEDGED: Yes
REVIEW PROCESS: External reviewers
NOTIFICATION TIME: 1 month

CRITICISM: Yes

ACCEPTANCE RATE: 90%
REVISION: Medium
EARLY PUBLICATION OPTION: No
COPYRIGHT POLICY: Publisher
FEE: None
REPRINTS: 5 or 6
PUBLICATION TIME LAG: 3 months
PROOFS: No
PAGE CHARGES: No

JOURNAL TITLE: Catholic Library World

SUBSCRIPTION ADDRESS: Catholic Library World, 461 West Lancaster Ave., Haverford, PA 19041

PRICE: $20
CIRCULATION: 4,000
AFFILIATION: Catholic Library Association
INDEXED/ABSTRACTED: BRI, Cerdic, CIJE, CPLI, LISA, LL, RBRI
FREQUENCY: 10 x a year

MANUSCRIPT ADDRESS: John T. Corrigan, Catholic Library World, 461 West Lancaster Ave., Haverford, PA 19041

EDITORIAL POLICY: Current information on a variety of topics of concern to the library profession

AUDIENCE: All professional librarians

PREFERRED TOPICS: Any and all topics dealing with libraries and information services

INAPPROPRIATE TOPICS: None

FEATURES: "Comment on"; all articles dealing with the specific theme of the issue

REVIEWS: Yes
STUDENT PAPERS: Yes

RESTRICTIONS: None
COVER LETTER: Yes
NUMBER OF COPIES: 2
STYLE: MLA
FORMAT: Standard
ABSTRACT: Yes
LENGTH: 2,200-2,500
INSTRUCTION FORM: Yes
(100)

ACKNOWLEDGED: Yes
REVIEW PROCESS: Editor
NOTIFICATION TIME: 2 weeks

CRITICISM: No

ACCEPTANCE RATE: 70%
REVISION: Light
EARLY PUBLICATION OPTION: Yes
COPYRIGHT POLICY: Not copyrighted; author may request copyright
FEE: None
REPRINTS: 100 if requested
PUBLICATION TIME LAG: 3 months
PROOFS:
PAGE CHARGES: No

**JOURNAL TITLE:** Children's Literature

**SUBSCRIPTION ADDRESS:** Customer Services, Yale University Press, 92A Yale Station, New Haven, CT 06520

**PRICE:** $7.95
**CIRCULATION:** Not given
**AFFILIATION:** Children's Literature Association; Modern Language Association
**INDEXED/ABSTRACTED:** MLA
**FREQUENCY:** Annual

**MANUSCRIPT ADDRESS:** Francelia Butler, Department of English, University of Connecticut, Storrs, CT. 06268

**EDITORIAL POLICY:** To seek out and select the best possible research in the field

**AUDIENCE:** Scholars interested in children's literature

**PREFERRED TOPICS:** Aspects, national and international, of children's literature

**INAPPROPRIATE TOPICS:** Not given

**FEATURES:** Dissertations of note, topics for research

**REVIEWS:** Yes     **STUDENT PAPERS:** Yes

**RESTRICTIONS:** None
**COVER LETTER:** Yes
**NUMBER OF COPIES:** 2
**STYLE:** MLA
**FORMAT:** Standard
**ABSTRACT:** No
**LENGTH:** 3,000-5,000
**INSTRUCTION FORM:** No

**ACKNOWLEDGED:** Yes
**REVIEW PROCESS:** External reviewers
**NOTIFICATION TIME:** 2-3 months

**CRITICISM:** Rarely

**ACCEPTANCE RATE:** 5%
**REVISION:** Depends on state of article
**EARLY PUBLICATION OPTION:** Not given
**COPYRIGHT POLICY:** Publisher
**FEE:** None
**REPRINTS:** 25 offprints
**PUBLICATION TIME LAG:** 1 year
**PROOFS:** Yes
**PAGE CHARGES:** No

JOURNAL TITLE: Children's Literature in Education
SUBSCRIPTION ADDRESS: Agathon Press, 15 East 26th St., New York, NY 10010

PRICE: $12
CIRCULATION: 3,000
AFFILIATION: None
INDEXED/ABSTRACTED: Not given

FREQUENCY: Quarterly

MANUSCRIPT ADDRESS: Joan W. Blos, 1725 South University, Ann Arbor, MI 48104

EDITORIAL POLICY: Seeks to promote lively discussion of books for children and young adults and to heighten professional awareness and understanding of this literature and its use
AUDIENCE: Librarians, teachers, writers, and concerned parents
PREFERRED TOPICS: Ind-depth studies of books and authors; reevaluation of classics; studies of books or authors deserving wider recognition; analytic reviews of recent books
INAPPROPRIATE TOPICS: Not given

FEATURES: Not given

REVIEWS: Not given

STUDENT PAPERS: Not given

RESTRICTIONS: None
COVER LETTER: Yes
NUMBER OF COPIES: 2
STYLE: MLA
FORMAT: Standard

ABSTRACT: Not given
LENGTH: 3,500
INSTRUCTION FORM: Not given

ACKNOWLEDGED: Not given
REVIEW PROCESS: Editorial board and external reviewers

NOTIFICATION TIME: Not given

CRITICISM: Not given

ACCEPTANCE RATE: Not given
REVISION: Medium
EARLY PUBLICATION OPTION: No
COPYRIGHT POLICY: Publisher
FEE: None
REPRINTS: Not given

PUBLICATION TIME LAG: 3-6 months
PROOFS: Yes
PAGE CHARGES: No

**JOURNAL TITLE:** Choice

**SUBSCRIPTION ADDRESS:** Subscription Department, CHOICE, 100 Riverview Center, Middletown, CT 06457

**PRICE:** $50
**CIRCULATION:** 6,000
**AFFILIATION:** Association of College and Research Libraries
**INDEXED/ABSTRACTED:** BRI

**FREQUENCY:** Monthly

**MANUSCRIPT ADDRESS:** Jay Martin Poole, CHOICE, 100 Riverview Center, Middletown, CT 06457

**EDITORIAL POLICY:** Review scholarly publications published in U.S. suitable for college libraries

**AUDIENCE:** Colleges and universities

**PREFERRED TOPICS:** Topics of interest to the college curriculum

**INAPPROPRIATE TOPICS:** Not given

**FEATURES:** Bibliographic essays, periodical review column

**REVIEWS:** Yes
**STUDENT PAPERS:** No

**RESTRICTIONS:** None
**COVER LETTER:** Yes
**NUMBER OF COPIES:** 1
**STYLE:** Not given
**FORMAT:** Standard
**ABSTRACT:** No
**LENGTH:** Not given
**INSTRUCTION FORM:** Yes

**ACKNOWLEDGED:** Yes
**REVIEW PROCESS:** Editorial board
**NOTIFICATION TIME:** 1 month

**CRITICISM:** No

**ACCEPTANCE RATE:** Not given
**REVISION:** Medium
**EARLY PUBLICATION OPTION:** No
**COPYRIGHT POLICY:** Publisher
**FEE:** None
**REPRINTS:** 6
**PUBLICATION TIME LAG:** 3 months
**PROOFS:** Yes
**PAGE CHARGES:** No

**JOURNAL TITLE:** The Christian Librarian

**SUBSCRIPTION ADDRESS:** Circulation Editor, The Christian Librarian, Cedarville College, Cedarville, OH 45314

**PRICE:** $4
**CIRCULATION:**
**AFFILIATION:** Christian Librarians' Fellowship
**INDEXED/ABSTRACTED:** ChPI

**FREQUENCY:** Quarterly

**MANUSCRIPT ADDRESS:** Ron Jordahl, Prairie Bible Institute Library, Three Hills, Alberta, T0M 2A0, Canada

**EDITORIAL POLICY:** A vehicle through which the members of the Christian Librarians' Fellowship can communicate their interpretation of their vocation.

**AUDIENCE:** Membership of the Christian Librarians' Fellowship

**PREFERRED TOPICS:** Christian interpretation of librarianship, theory, philosophy, and practice of library science. Bibliographic articles, human interest stories relating to books, libraries, and librarians.

**INAPPROPRIATE TOPICS:** Not given

**FEATURES:** Not given

**REVIEWS:** Yes         **STUDENT PAPERS:** Yes

**RESTRICTIONS:** None
**COVER LETTER:** Yes
**NUMBER OF COPIES:** 1
**STYLE:** Not given
**FORMAT:** Standard

**ABSTRACT:** No
**LENGTH:** 3,500
**INSTRUCTION FORM:** Yes

**ACKNOWLEDGED:** Yes
**REVIEW PROCESS:** Editorial board

**NOTIFICATION TIME:** 2 weeks

**CRITICISM:** Yes

**ACCEPTANCE RATE:** 75%
**REVISION:** Light
**EARLY PUBLICATION OPTION:** Not given
**COPYRIGHT POLICY:** Publisher
**FEE:** None
**REPRINTS:** 1

**PUBLICATION TIME LAG:** 18 months
**PROOFS:** No

**PAGE CHARGES:** Not given

**JOURNAL TITLE:** Church & Synagogue Libraries

**SUBSCRIPTION ADDRESS:** Church and Synagogue Libraries, P.O. Box 1130, Bryn Mawr, PA 19101

**PRICE:** $7.50
**FREQUENCY:** Bimonthly
**CIRCULATION:** 2,400
**AFFILIATION:** Church and Synagogue Library Association
**INDEXED/ABSTRACTED:** ChPI

**MANUSCRIPT ADDRESS:** Church and Synagogue Libraries, P.O. Box 1130, Bryn Mawr, PA 19101

**EDITORIAL POLICY:** Official bulletin of CSLA, reports activities; train and inspire congregational librarians

**AUDIENCE:** Members of CSLA and other interested librarians

**PREFERRED TOPICS:** Those that deal with the conduct of libraries in local churches and synagogues

**INAPPROPRIATE TOPICS:** Not given

**FEATURES:** Stories of successful operations in local church or synagogue libraries; new ideas and instructions in methods for volunteer librarians.

**REVIEWS:** Yes     **STUDENT PAPERS:** No

**RESTRICTIONS:** None
**COVER LETTER:** Yes
**NUMBER OF COPIES:** 1
**STYLE:** Standard
**FORMAT:** Standard
**ABSTRACT:** No
**LENGTH:** 200-1,500
**INSTRUCTION FORM:** Yes

**ACKNOWLEDGED:** Yes     **NOTIFICATION TIME:** 2 weeks
**REVIEW PROCESS:** Executive Board of CSLA

**CRITICISM:** No

**ACCEPTANCE RATE:** 80%
**REVISION:** Medium
**EARLY PUBLICATION OPTION:** No
**COPYRIGHT POLICY:** Not copyrighted
**FEE:** None
**REPRINTS:** As many as requested
**PUBLICATION TIME LAG:** 3-6 months
**PROOFS:** Not unless requested
**PAGE CHARGES:** No

ALPHABETICAL LISTING OF JOURNALS / 61

JOURNAL TITLE: The Classification Society Bulletin

SUBSCRIPTION ADDRESS: Department of Microbiology, University of Leicester, University Rd., Leicester LE1 7RH England

PRICE: $5
FREQUENCY: Annual
CIRCULATION: 500
AFFILIATION: The Classification Society
INDEXED/ABSTRACTED: LISA

MANUSCRIPT ADDRESS: Department of Microbiology, University of Leicester, University Road, Leicester LE1 7RH England

EDITORIAL POLICY: Any contributions to theory or practice of classification

AUDIENCE: Information scientists, librarians, statisticians, taxonomists, those working in classification
PREFERRED TOPICS: Theory and practice of classification

INAPPROPRIATE TOPICS: Not given

FEATURES: Brief reports of meetings, and news items for members

REVIEWS: Yes
STUDENT PAPERS: No

RESTRICTIONS: None
COVER LETTER: Yes
NUMBER OF COPIES: 2
STYLE: Not given
FORMAT: Standard
ABSTRACT: No
LENGTH: 2,000
INSTRUCTION FORM: No

ACKNOWLEDGED: Yes
REVIEW PROCESS: External reviewers
NOTIFICATION TIME: 1-2 months

CRITICISM: Yes

ACCEPTANCE RATE: Not given
REVISION: Light
EARLY PUBLICATION OPTION: No
COPYRIGHT POLICY: Publisher
FEE: None
REPRINTS: 25
PUBLICATION TIME LAG: 3-15 months
PROOFS: No
PAGE CHARGES: No

**JOURNAL TITLE:** Collection Building

**SUBSCRIPTION ADDRESS:** Gaylord Professional Publications, Box 4901, Syracuse, NY 13221

**PRICE:** $55
**CIRCULATION:** Not given
**AFFILIATION:** Not given
**INDEXED/ABSTRACTED:** LL

**FREQUENCY:** 3 x a year

**MANUSCRIPT ADDRESS:** Gaylord Professional Publications, Box 4901, Syracuse, NY 13221

**EDITORIAL POLICY:** To promote excellence in collection development through the publication of studies in the development and effective use of library resources.

**AUDIENCE:** Librarians, library school faculty and students

**PREFERRED TOPICS:** Theoretical and practical aspects of effective collection development

**INAPPROPRIATE TOPICS:** Not given

**FEATURES:** Research-based analyses of specific aspects of collection building

**REVIEWS:** Not given

**STUDENT PAPERS:** Yes

**RESTRICTIONS:** None
**COVER LETTER:** Yes
**NUMBER OF COPIES:** 1
**STYLE:** Chicago
**FORMAT:** Standard

**ABSTRACT:** No
**LENGTH:** 5,000-7,500
**INSTRUCTION FORM:** Yes

**ACKNOWLEDGED:** Yes
**REVIEW PROCESS:** Editorial board

**NOTIFICATION TIME:** 1-3 months

**CRITICISM:** No

**ACCEPTANCE RATE:** 25%
**REVISION:** Medium
**EARLY PUBLICATION OPTION:** No
**COPYRIGHT POLICY:** Publisher
**FEE:** $50-$150 upon publication
**REPRINTS:** Not given

**PUBLICATION TIME LAG:** 3-6 months
**PROOFS:** No
**PAGE CHARGES:** No

JOURNAL TITLE: Collection Management

SUBSCRIPTION ADDRESS: Haworth Press, 28 East 22 Street, New York, NY 10010

PRICE: $48
CIRCULATION: 1,000
AFFILIATION: None
INDEXED/ABSTRACTED: LL

FREQUENCY: Quarterly

MANUSCRIPT ADDRESS: Jasper Schad, Collection Management, Wichita State University, Wichita, KS 67208

EDITORIAL POLICY: To disseminate information relating to the theories, practices and research findings involved with the management of library collections

AUDIENCE: Library researchers, administrators, educators, students and practitioners

PREFERRED TOPICS: Management, weeding, secondary storage, resource sharing, budget allocation, collection development

INAPPROPRIATE TOPICS: Not given

FEATURES: Tutorials and suggestions for classics

REVIEWS: None

STUDENT PAPERS: Yes

RESTRICTIONS: None
COVER LETTER: Yes
NUMBER OF COPIES: 3
STYLE: Chicago
FORMAT: Not given

ABSTRACT: 100
LENGTH: 15 pages
INSTRUCTION FORM: Yes

ACKNOWLEDGED: Yes
REVIEW PROCESS: External reviewers

NOTIFICATION TIME: 3 months

CRITICISM: Yes

ACCEPTANCE RATE: 75%
REVISION: Medium
EARLY PUBLICATION OPTION: Yes
COPYRIGHT POLICY: Publisher
FEE: None
REPRINTS: 10

PUBLICATION TIME LAG: 4-6 months
PROOFS: Yes
PAGE CHARGES: No

**JOURNAL TITLE:** College & Research Libraries
**SUBSCRIPTION ADDRESS:** American Library Association, 50 E. Huron Street, Chicago, IL 60611

**PRICE:** $25
**FREQUENCY:** Bimonthly
**CIRCULATION:** 12,000
**AFFILIATION:** Association of College & Research Libraries
**INDEXED/ABSTRACTED:** CC, CIJE, ISA, LISA, LL

**MANUSCRIPT ADDRESS:** Richard D. Johnson, James M. Milne Library, State University College, Oneonta, NY 13820

**EDITORIAL POLICY:** A medium for professional communication among academic and research librarians

**AUDIENCE:** Academic and research librarians
**PREFERRED TOPICS:** Any which relate to academic librarianship

**INAPPROPRIATE TOPICS:** Not given

**FEATURES:** Sem-annual review of new reference works

**REVIEWS:** Yes
**STUDENT PAPERS:** Not given

**RESTRICTIONS:** None
**COVER LETTER:** Yes
**NUMBER OF COPIES:** 2
**STYLE:** Chicago
**FORMAT:** Standard
**ABSTRACT:** 75-100
**LENGTH:** 1,000-1,500
**INSTRUCTION FORM:** See journal

**ACKNOWLEDGED:** Yes
**REVIEW PROCESS:** Editorial board and external reviewers
**NOTIFICATION TIME:** 6-8 weeks

**CRITICISM:** Yes

**ACCEPTANCE RATE:** 25-33%
**REVISION:** Not given
**EARLY PUBLICATION OPTION:** Not given
**COPYRIGHT POLICY:** Publisher
**FEE:** None
**REPRINTS:** 25
**PUBLICATION TIME LAG:** 6-8 months
**PROOFS:** Yes
**PAGE CHARGES:** No

JOURNAL TITLE: College & Research Libraries News

SUBSCRIPTION ADDRESS: College & Research Libraries News, A.L.A., 50 East Huron Street, Chicago, IL 60611

PRICE: $5
CIRCULATION: 11,000
AFFILIATION: Association of College and Research Libraries
INDEXED/ABSTRACTED: CC, CIJE, ISA, LL, SSCI

FREQUENCY: 11 x a year

MANUSCRIPT ADDRESS: C. James Schmidt, College and Research Libraries News, c/o Research Libraries Group, Jordan Quadrangle, Stanford University, Stanford, CA 94305

EDITORIAL POLICY: Official news publication of the Association of College and Research Libraries, and a clearing house for news about academic librarianship

AUDIENCE: Academic librarians

PREFERRED TOPICS: National news relating to academic librarianship, personnel changes in libraries, continuing education for librarians, notable activities in academic libraries

INAPPROPRIATE TOPICS: Not given

FEATURES: Professional survival column on career development in academic libraries, vocations feature-profiles of the vocations within academic librarianship

REVIEWS: No

STUDENT PAPERS: No

RESTRICTIONS: None
COVER LETTER: No
NUMBER OF COPIES: 1
STYLE: Not given
FORMAT: Not given

ABSTRACT: No
LENGTH: 500-1,000
INSTRUCTION FORM: No

ACKNOWLEDGED: Yes
REVIEW PROCESS: Editor

NOTIFICATION TIME: 1 week

CRITICISM: Yes

ACCEPTANCE RATE: 80%
REVISION: Heavy
EARLY PUBLICATION OPTION: No
COPYRIGHT POLICY: Publisher
FEE: None
REPRINTS: None

PUBLICATION TIME LAG: 6 weeks
PROOFS: No

PAGE CHARGES: No

**JOURNAL TITLE:** Computers and the Humanities

**SUBSCRIPTION ADDRESS:** North-Holland Publishing Company, P.O. Box 103, 1000AC Amsterdam, Netherlands

**PRICE:** $15
**CIRCULATION:** 1,200
**AFFILIATION:** Association for Computers and the Humanities
**INDEXED/ABSTRACTED:** AES, CR, MLA, SSCI, LLBA
**FREQUENCY:** Quarterly

**MANUSCRIPT ADDRESS:** Joseph Raben, Queens College, Flushing, NY 11367

**EDITORIAL POLICY:** Reports on computer-aided research (including indexing and information retrieval) in the humanities

**AUDIENCE:** Scholars in the field

**PREFERRED TOPICS:** Computer-aided research in the humanities.

**INAPPROPRIATE TOPICS:** Not given

**FEATURES:** Reports from research institutes, many book reviews, abstracts of articles from other journals

**REVIEWS:** Yes, solicited only  **STUDENT PAPERS:** No

**RESTRICTIONS:** None
**COVER LETTER:** Yes
**NUMBER OF COPIES:** 4
**STYLE:** MLA
**FORMAT:** Standard
**ABSTRACT:** No
**LENGTH:** 2,000-2,500
**INSTRUCTION FORM:** Yes

**ACKNOWLEDGED:** Yes
**REVIEW PROCESS:** External reviewers
**NOTIFICATION TIME:** 6 months

**CRITICISM:** Yes

**ACCEPTANCE RATE:** 65%
**REVISION:** Medium
**EARLY PUBLICATION OPTION:** No
**COPYRIGHT POLICY:** Publisher
**FEE:** None
**REPRINTS:** 50
**PUBLICATION TIME LAG:** 6 months
**PROOFS:** Yes
**PAGE CHARGES:** No

**JOURNAL TITLE:** Conservation Administration News

**SUBSCRIPTION ADDRESS:** Box 3334, University Station, Laramie, WY 82071

**PRICE:** $12
**CIRCULATION:** 250
**AFFILIATION:** University of Wyoming Libraries
**INDEXED/ABSTRACTED:** Not given
**FREQUENCY:** Quarterly

**MANUSCRIPT ADDRESS:** Box 3334, University Station, Laramie, WY 82071

**EDITORIAL POLICY:** Information on preservation matters for the library and archival communities

**AUDIENCE:** Library and archival communities

**PREFERRED TOPICS:** Anything dealing with preservation

**INAPPROPRIATE TOPICS:** Not given

**FEATURES:** Articles on specific preservation operations in any institution or private setting, biographical pieces on conservators, etc.

**REVIEWS:** Yes
**STUDENT PAPERS:** No

**RESTRICTIONS:** None
**COVER LETTER:** Yes
**NUMBER OF COPIES:** 1
**STYLE:** MLA or Chicago
**FORMAT:** Standard
**ABSTRACT:** Not given
**LENGTH:** 1,500
**INSTRUCTION FORM:** Not given

**ACKNOWLEDGED:** Yes
**REVIEW PROCESS:** Editorial board
**NOTIFICATION TIME:** 1-2 months

**CRITICISM:** No

**ACCEPTANCE RATE:** 90%+
**REVISION:** Medium
**EARLY PUBLICATION OPTION:** No
**COPYRIGHT POLICY:** Not copyrighted
**FEE:** None
**REPRINTS:** None
**PUBLICATION TIME LAG:** 6 months
**PROOFS:** No
**PAGE CHARGES:** No

**JOURNAL TITLE:** Current Studies in Librarianship

**SUBSCRIPTION ADDRESS:** Prefer the order be submitted through a periodical jobber

**PRICE:** $5
**CIRCULATION:** 600
**AFFILIATION:** Graduate Library School, University of R.I.
**INDEXED/ABSTRACTED:** LL
**FREQUENCY:** Annual

**MANUSCRIPT ADDRESS:** L. B. Woods, University of R.I., Graduate Library School, Kingston, RI 02881

**EDITORIAL POLICY:** Subjects of general interest to librarians. Should be readable, timely, and contain new information or approach known information with new insight.

**AUDIENCE:** All librarians

**PREFERRED TOPICS:** General articles on any topic of interest

**INAPPROPRIATE TOPICS:** How we did it articles

**FEATURES:** Not given

**REVIEWS:** No

**STUDENT PAPERS:** Yes

**RESTRICTIONS:** None
**COVER LETTER:** Yes
**NUMBER OF COPIES:** 1
**STYLE:** Turabian
**FORMAT:** Standard
**ABSTRACT:** No
**LENGTH:** 8-15 pages
**INSTRUCTION FORM:** Yes

**ACKNOWLEDGED:** Yes
**REVIEW PROCESS:** Editorial board
**NOTIFICATION TIME:** 4-6 weeks

**CRITICISM:** Usually

**ACCEPTANCE RATE:** 50%
**REVISION:** Heavy
**EARLY PUBLICATION OPTION:** No
**COPYRIGHT POLICY:** Publisher
**FEE:** None
**REPRINTS:** 3 copies of issue
**PUBLICATION TIME LAG:** Less than 1 year
**PROOFS:** No
**PAGE CHARGES:** No

**JOURNAL TITLE:** Data Management

**SUBSCRIPTION ADDRESS:** 505 Busse Highway, Park Ridge, IL 60068

**PRICE:** $16
**CIRCULATION:** 33,000
**AFFILIATION:** Data Processing Management Association
**INDEXED/ABSTRACTED:** Not given

**FREQUENCY:** Monthly

**MANUSCRIPT ADDRESS:** 505 Busse Highway, Park Ridge, IL 60068

**EDITORIAL POLICY:** Industry related articles, advertising, book reviews

**AUDIENCE:** Data processing management level personnel

**PREFERRED TOPICS:** Research articles, case studies, commentaries, review articles and any topics relating to data processing

**INAPPROPRIATE TOPICS:** Not given

**FEATURES:** Hardware and software usage, personnel and general management

**REVIEWS:** Not given
**STUDENT PAPERS:** Yes

**RESTRICTIONS:** None
**COVER LETTER:** Yes
**NUMBER OF COPIES:** 1
**STYLE:** Not given
**FORMAT:** Standard
**ABSTRACT:** No
**LENGTH:** 2,000
**INSTRUCTION FORM:** Yes

**ACKNOWLEDGED:** Yes
**REVIEW PROCESS:** Editorial board
**NOTIFICATION TIME:** 10-12 weeks

**CRITICISM:** Yes

**ACCEPTANCE RATE:** 75%
**REVISION:** Medium
**EARLY PUBLICATION OPTION:** No
**COPYRIGHT POLICY:** Publisher
**FEE:** None
**REPRINTS:** 6
**PUBLICATION TIME LAG:** 4-5 months
**PROOFS:** No
**PAGE CHARGES:** No

**JOURNAL TITLE:** Database Magazine
**SUBSCRIPTION ADDRESS:** 11 Tannery Lane, Weston, CT 06883

**PRICE:** $52
**CIRCULATION:** 2,000
**AFFILIATION:** None
**INDEXED/ABSTRACTED:** INSPEC, LISA, MI, CIJE
**FREQUENCY:** Quarterly

**MANUSCRIPT ADDRESS:** J. K. Pemberton, 11 Tannery Lane, Weston, CT 06883

**EDITORIAL POLICY:** Practical, how-to articles on searching online data bases

**AUDIENCE:** Librarians and other online searchers

**PREFERRED TOPICS:** Practical articles telling how to use specific databases; lots of actual examples

**INAPPROPRIATE TOPICS:** Not given

**FEATURES:** None

**REVIEWS:** No
**STUDENT PAPERS:** No

**RESTRICTIONS:** None
**COVER LETTER:** Yes
**NUMBER OF COPIES:** 3
**STYLE:** House
**FORMAT:** Standard
**ABSTRACT:** No
**LENGTH:** 2,000-3,000
**INSTRUCTION FORM:** Yes

**ACKNOWLEDGED:** Yes
**REVIEW PROCESS:** External reviewers
**NOTIFICATION TIME:** 1-2 months

**CRITICISM:** Yes

**ACCEPTANCE RATE:** 90%
**REVISION:** Light
**EARLY PUBLICATION OPTION:** No
**COPYRIGHT POLICY:** Publisher
**FEE:** $100-$300 after publication
**REPRINTS:** 20
**PUBLICATION TIME LAG:** 3-4 months
**PROOFS:** Yes
**PAGE CHARGES:** No

**JOURNAL TITLE:** Documents to the People

**SUBSCRIPTION ADDRESS:** Government Documents Round Table, American Library Association, 50 E. Huron St., Chicago, IL 60611

**PRICE:** $15
**FREQUENCY:** Bimonthly
**CIRCULATION:** 2,000
**AFFILIATION:** Government Documents Round Table
**INDEXED/ABSTRACTED:** Not

**MANUSCRIPT ADDRESS:** LeRoy C. Schwarzkopf, McKeldin Library, University of Maryland, College Park, MD 20742

**EDITORIAL POLICY:** News about activities including minutes and report of semi-annual meetings. Also current information on government publications and related government activities
**AUDIENCE:** Documents librarians and other librarians who work with government publications
**PREFERRED TOPICS:** Current developments or events related to the publishing and distribution of government documents

**INAPPROPRIATE TOPICS:** Not given

**FEATURES:** Reports of meetings, workshops, and conferences; related activities by other organizations and groups

**REVIEWS:** No
**STUDENT PAPERS:** No

**RESTRICTIONS:** None
**COVER LETTER:** Yes
**NUMBER OF COPIES:** 1
**STYLE:** Not given
**FORMAT:** Standard
**ABSTRACT:** No
**LENGTH:** 2,500
**INSTRUCTION FORM:** Yes

**ACKNOWLEDGED:** Yes
**REVIEW PROCESS:** Editorial board
**NOTIFICATION TIME:** 1 month

**CRITICISM:** No

**ACCEPTANCE RATE:** 80%
**REVISION:** Light
**EARLY PUBLICATION OPTION:** No
**COPYRIGHT POLICY:** Not copyrighted
**FEE:** None
**REPRINTS:** None
**PUBLICATION TIME LAG:** 1-3 months
**PROOFS:** No
**PAGE CHARGES:** No

**JOURNAL TITLE:** Drexel Library Quarterly

**SUBSCRIPTION ADDRESS:** Drexel Library Quarterly, School of Library and Information Science, Drexel University, Philadelphia, PA 19104

**PRICE:** $12
**CIRCULATION:** 1,200
**AFFILIATION:** None
**INDEXED/ABSTRACTED:** BRI, CALL, CC, CIJE, ISA, LL, PAIS, SSCI

**FREQUENCY:** Quarterly

**MANUSCRIPT ADDRESS:** Drexel Library Quarterly, School of Library and Information Science, Drexel University, Philadelphia, PA 19104

**EDITORIAL POLICY:** Each issue highlights a topic of current concern to library and information professionals

**AUDIENCE:** Library and information science professionals

**PREFERRED TOPICS:** Varies depending on the focus of the individual issue

**INAPPROPRIATE TOPICS:** No unsolicited manuscripts are accepted

**FEATURES:** Guest editor, who is a specialist in the topic area, is invited to prepare a proposal for the issue

**REVIEWS:** No  **STUDENT PAPERS:** No

**RESTRICTIONS:** None
**COVER LETTER:** Yes
**NUMBER OF COPIES:** 2
**STYLE:** Chicago
**FORMAT:** Standard

**ABSTRACT:** No
**LENGTH:** 4,000-5,000
**INSTRUCTION FORM:** Yes

**ACKNOWLEDGED:** Yes
**REVIEW PROCESS:** Editorial board and issue and managing editors

**NOTIFICATION TIME:** 2-3 months

**CRITICISM:** No

**ACCEPTANCE RATE:** 90%
**REVISION:** Medium
**EARLY PUBLICATION OPTION:** No
**COPYRIGHT POLICY:** Publisher
**FEE:** None
**REPRINTS:** 5

**PUBLICATION TIME LAG:** Varies
**PROOFS:** No
**PAGE CHARGES:** No

**JOURNAL TITLE:** Education Libraries

**SUBSCRIPTION ADDRESS:** Judith Segur, 101 Brookfield Road, Tewksbury, MA 01876

**PRICE:** $5
**CIRCULATION:** 500
**AFFILIATION:** Special Libraries Association Education Division
**INDEXED/ABSTRACTED:** Not

**FREQUENCY:** Quarterly

**MANUSCRIPT ADDRESS:** Guest Perry, Education Libraries, Houghton Mifflin Co., One Beacon St., Boston, MA 02107

**EDITORIAL POLICY:** Each issue has a specific theme

**AUDIENCE:** Librarians in education libraries

**PREFERRED TOPICS:** Research articles on topics of interest to librarians in special libraries

**INAPPROPRIATE TOPICS:** Not given

**FEATURES:** What's new in ERIC; special issues of journals

**REVIEWS:** Yes

**STUDENT PAPERS:** No

**RESTRICTIONS:** None
**COVER LETTER:** Yes
**NUMBER OF COPIES:** 2
**STYLE:** Chicago
**FORMAT:** Standard

**ABSTRACT:** No
**LENGTH:** 800
**INSTRUCTION FORM:** Not given

**ACKNOWLEDGED:** Yes
**REVIEW PROCESS:** Editors

**NOTIFICATION TIME:** 2 weeks

**CRITICISM:** No

**ACCEPTANCE RATE:** 90%
**REVISION:** Varies
**EARLY PUBLICATION OPTION:** No
**COPYRIGHT POLICY:** Not copyrighted
**FEE:** None
**REPRINTS:** 3 or 4 copies of issue

**PUBLICATION TIME LAG:** 3 months
**PROOFS:** If possible
**PAGE CHARGES:** No

**JOURNAL TITLE:** Educational Technology

**SUBSCRIPTION ADDRESS:** 140 Sylvan Avenue, Englewood Cliffs, NJ 07632

**PRICE:** $49
**CIRCULATION:** 5,000
**AFFILIATION:** None
**INDEXED/ABSTRACTED:** CIJE, ECER, EEA, EdI, PA

**FREQUENCY:** Monthly

**MANUSCRIPT ADDRESS:** Lawrence Lipsitz, 140 Sylvan Avenue, Englewood Cliffs, NJ 07632

**EDITORIAL POLICY:** Complete coverage of the field of educational technology, broadly defined

**AUDIENCE:** Educators, trainers, designers of instruction, professors of education

**PREFERRED TOPICS:** Essays interpreting applications of scientific knowledge and research in educational practice

**INAPPROPRIATE TOPICS:** Formal research studies; this is not a classical research journal

**FEATURES:** Work-in-progress

**REVIEWS:** No

**STUDENT PAPERS:** Yes

**RESTRICTIONS:** None
**COVER LETTER:** Yes
**NUMBER OF COPIES:** 2
**STYLE:** House
**FORMAT:** Standard

**ABSTRACT:** No
**LENGTH:** 3,000
**INSTRUCTION FORM:** Yes

**ACKNOWLEDGED:** No
**REVIEW PROCESS:** Editorial board

**NOTIFICATION TIME:** 14 days

**CRITICISM:** Sometimes

**ACCEPTANCE RATE:** 25%
**REVISION:** Medium
**EARLY PUBLICATION OPTION:** No
**COPYRIGHT POLICY:** Publisher
**FEE:** None
**REPRINTS:** None

**PUBLICATION TIME LAG:** 6 months
**PROOFS:** Yes
**PAGE CHARGES:** No

JOURNAL TITLE: Emergency Librarian

SUBSCRIPTION ADDRESS: Dyad Services, P.O. Box 4696, Station C., London, Ontario N5W 5L7

PRICE: $10
CIRCULATION: 1,400
AFFILIATION: None
INDEXED/ABSTRACTED: LL

FREQUENCY: Bimonthly

MANUSCRIPT ADDRESS: Dyad Services, P.O. Box 46258, Station G, Vancouver, BC V6R 4G0

EDITORIAL POLICY: To improve library service for children and young adults in school and public libraries

AUDIENCE: Youth librarians in school and public libraries

PREFERRED TOPICS: Those which will help to improve service for children and young adults; practical goal oriented articles; strategies for change/improvement

INAPPROPRIATE TOPICS: Not given

FEATURES: 5 theme issues per year, books for liberated kids, evaluations of libraries

REVIEWS: Yes

STUDENT PAPERS: Yes

RESTRICTIONS: None
COVER LETTER: Yes
NUMBER OF COPIES: 2
STYLE: Not given
FORMAT: Standard

ABSTRACT: No
LENGTH: 1,500
INSTRUCTION FORM: Yes

ACKNOWLEDGED: Yes
REVIEW PROCESS: External reviewers

NOTIFICATION TIME: 4 weeks

CRITICISM: No

ACCEPTANCE RATE: 75%
REVISION: Medium
EARLY PUBLICATION OPTION: No
COPYRIGHT POLICY: Publisher
FEE: $25 on publication
REPRINTS: 2

PUBLICATION TIME LAG: maximum of 10 months
PROOFS: No
PAGE CHARGES: No

JOURNAL TITLE: Film Library Quarterly
SUBSCRIPTION ADDRESS: Box 348, Radio City Station, N. Y., NY 10019

PRICE: $12
CIRCULATION: 2,000
AFFILIATION: Film Library Information Council
INDEXED/ABSTRACTED: FLI, IIFP, LL

FREQUENCY: Quarterly

MANUSCRIPT ADDRESS: Editor, Film Library Quarterly, Box 348, Radio City Station, N. Y., NY 10019

EDITORIAL POLICY: To provide information and ideas that will promote the wider and more effective use of films and non-print media by public libraries and the communities they serve
AUDIENCE: Public librarians

PREFERRED TOPICS: Non-commercial cinema and video and their application in libraries

INAPPROPRIATE TOPICS: Not given

FEATURES: Articles on documentary filmmakers and their work

REVIEWS: Yes          STUDENT PAPERS: Yes

RESTRICTIONS: None
COVER LETTER: Yes
NUMBER OF COPIES: 1
STYLE: House
FORMAT: Standard

ABSTRACT: No
LENGTH: No limit
INSTRUCTION FORM: Yes

ACKNOWLEDGED: Yes
REVIEW PROCESS: Editors

NOTIFICATION TIME: 1-6 weeks

CRITICISM: No

ACCEPTANCE RATE: 80%
REVISION: Varies
EARLY PUBLICATION OPTION: No
COPYRIGHT POLICY: Publisher
FEE: None
REPRINTS: 10 copies of issue

PUBLICATION TIME LAG: 6-12 months
PROOFS: Yes
PAGE CHARGES: No

JOURNAL TITLE: Focus on International and Comparative Librarianship

SUBSCRIPTION ADDRESS: International and Comparative Librarianship Group, Library Association, 7 Ridgmount St., London WC1E 7AE, England

PRICE: $7.50　　FREQUENCY: Quarterly
CIRCULATION: 1,750
AFFILIATION: LA. International and Comparative Librarianship Group
INDEXED/ABSTRACTED: LISA, RZ

MANUSCRIPT ADDRESS: Gordon Harris, Library, School of Slavonic & East European Studies, London WC1E 7HU, England

EDITORIAL POLICY: Includes material on all aspects of international librarianship and reports on research in comparative library systems in different countries

AUDIENCE: Librarians

PREFERRED TOPICS: Movements of librarians around the world; development of international systems and standards in librarianship; comparative studies

INAPPROPRIATE TOPICS: Descriptive articles on libraries abroad

FEATURES: Themes, e.g., UAP; Area studies

REVIEWS: Yes　　STUDENT PAPERS: No

RESTRICTIONS: None
COVER LETTER: Yes
NUMBER OF COPIES: 2
STYLE: Not given
FORMAT: Standard
ABSTRACT: Desirable
LENGTH: 1,500-2,000
INSTRUCTION FORM: No

ACKNOWLEDGED: Not given
REVIEW PROCESS: Not given
NOTIFICATION TIME: 1 month

CRITICISM: No

ACCEPTANCE RATE: 70%
REVISION: Medium
EARLY PUBLICATION OPTION: No
COPYRIGHT POLICY: Publisher
FEE: None
REPRINTS: 10 copies of issue
PUBLICATION TIME LAG: 2-5 months
PROOFS: No
PAGE CHARGES: No

**JOURNAL TITLE:** Fontes Artis Musicae

**SUBSCRIPTION ADDRESS:** Don L. Roberts, Music Library, Northwestern University, Evanston, IL 60201

**PRICE:** $18
**CIRCULATION:** 1,700
**AFFILIATION:** International Association of Music Libraries
**INDEXED/ABSTRACTED:** LISA, LL, MuI, RILM
**FREQUENCY:** Quarterly

**MANUSCRIPT ADDRESS:** Rita Benton, School of Music, University of Iowa, Iowa City, IA 52242

**EDITORIAL POLICY:** Articles and shorter items of interest to music librarians, as well as to the users of music libraries

**AUDIENCE:** Music librarians, general librarians and musicians

**PREFERRED TOPICS:** Tools and source materials collected by music libraries, or about organization and function of those libraries

**INAPPROPRIATE TOPICS:** Not given

**FEATURES:** Reviews of reference and bibliographical material used in music libraries; news items, communications

**REVIEWS:** Yes
**STUDENT PAPERS:** Yes

**RESTRICTIONS:** None
**COVER LETTER:** Yes
**NUMBER OF COPIES:** 2
**STYLE:** Not given
**FORMAT:** Standard
**ABSTRACT:** 50-100
**LENGTH:** 2-20 pages
**INSTRUCTION FORM:** Yes

**ACKNOWLEDGED:** Yes
**REVIEW PROCESS:** External reviewers
**NOTIFICATION TIME:** 2 weeks

**CRITICISM:** Usually

**ACCEPTANCE RATE:** 80%
**REVISION:** Medium
**EARLY PUBLICATION OPTION:** No
**COPYRIGHT POLICY:** Publisher
**FEE:** None
**REPRINTS:** 10
**PUBLICATION TIME LAG:** 3 months +
**PROOFS:** Yes
**PAGE CHARGES:** No

JOURNAL TITLE: Footnotes

SUBSCRIPTION ADDRESS: Footnotes, c/o Paula Murphy, Governors State University Library, Park Forest South, IL 60466

PRICE: Membership only  
CIRCULATION: 1,400  
AFFILIATION: Junior Members Roundtable, ALA  
INDEXED/ABSTRACTED: Not

FREQUENCY: Quarterly

MANUSCRIPT ADDRESS: Footnotes, Paula Murphy, Governors State University Library, Park Forest South, IL 60466

EDITORIAL POLICY: A newsletter of the Junior Members Roundtable

AUDIENCE: Junior members of the American Library Association

PREFERRED TOPICS: Topics helpful in getting the new librarian involved in the field of librarianship

INAPPROPRIATE TOPICS: Not given

FEATURES: No

REVIEWS: No

STUDENT PAPERS: No

RESTRICTIONS: Yes, members of JMRT  
COVER LETTER: No  
NUMBER OF COPIES: 1  
STYLE: Not given  
FORMAT: Standard

ABSTRACT: No  
LENGTH: 250  
INSTRUCTION FORM: No

ACKNOWLEDGED: No  
REVIEW PROCESS: Not applicable

NOTIFICATION TIME:

CRITICISM: Not applicable

ACCEPTANCE RATE: 100%  
REVISION: None  
EARLY PUBLICATION OPTION: No  
COPYRIGHT POLICY: Not copyrighted  
FEE: None  
REPRINTS: None

PUBLICATION TIME LAG: 6 weeks  
PROOFS: No

PAGE CHARGES: No

**JOURNAL TITLE:** Horn Book Magazine

**SUBSCRIPTION ADDRESS:** Horn Book Magazine, Circulation Department, Park Square Building, 31 St. James Avenue, Boston, MA 02116

**PRICE:** $18
**CIRCULATION:** 23,000
**AFFILIATION:** None
**INDEXED/ABSTRACTED:** BRD, BRI, CIJE, LL

**FREQUENCY:** Bimonthly

**MANUSCRIPT ADDRESS:** Ethel Heins, Horn Book, 585 Boylston St., Boston, MA 02116

**EDITORIAL POLICY:** A magazine entirely devoted to children's and young adult books

**AUDIENCE:** Librarians, teachers, parents, booksellers, editors, authors, illustrators, and children

**PREFERRED TOPICS:** Articles on all aspects of children's literature

**INAPPROPRIATE TOPICS:** Unsolicited book reviews, children's writing, personal anecdotes

**FEATURES:** "The Hunt Breakfast," Views on Science Books, The Outlook Tower, Letter from England, A Second Look, For Spanish Readers

**REVIEWS:** Yes

**STUDENT PAPERS:** No

**RESTRICTIONS:** No
**COVER LETTER:** Yes
**NUMBER OF COPIES:** 1
**STYLE:** Skillin
**FORMAT:** Standard

**ABSTRACT:** No
**LENGTH:** 2,500
**INSTRUCTION FORM:** Yes

**ACKNOWLEDGED:** Yes
**REVIEW PROCESS:** Editorial board

**NOTIFICATION TIME:** 2-4 months

**CRITICISM:** No

**ACCEPTANCE RATE:** 10%
**REVISION:** Medium
**EARLY PUBLICATION OPTION:** No
**COPYRIGHT POLICY:** Publisher
**FEE:** $20 per magazine page; $10 if article was a speech
**REPRINTS:** 2 copies of issue

**PUBLICATION TIME LAG:** 1 year
**PROOFS:** Yes
**PAGE CHARGES:** No

**JOURNAL TITLE:** IEEE Transactions on Information Theory

**SUBSCRIPTION ADDRESS:** IEEE Service Center, 445 Hoes Lane, Piscataway, NJ 08854

**PRICE:** $53
**CIRCULATION:** 5,000
**AFFILIATION:** Institute of Electrical and Electronics Engineers
**INDEXED/ABSTRACTED:** EnI
**FREQUENCY:** Bimonthly

**MANUSCRIPT ADDRESS:** N.J.A. Sloane, Bell Labs--Room 2C363, Murray Hill, NJ 07974

**EDITORIAL POLICY:** A theoretical journal dedicated to mathematical principles governing systems designed to transmit, manipulate, or utilize information

**AUDIENCE:** Communications engineers

**PREFERRED TOPICS:** Research articles, reviews, case studies on topics such as communication, coding, signal processing, pattern recognition, and learning

**INAPPROPRIATE TOPICS:** Not given

**FEATURES:** Theoretical and experimental papers concerned with the transmission, processing and utilization of information

**REVIEWS:** Yes
**STUDENT PAPERS:** Yes

**RESTRICTIONS:** None
**COVER LETTER:** Yes
**NUMBER OF COPIES:** 3
**STYLE:** see current issue
**FORMAT:** Standard
**ABSTRACT:** 200
**LENGTH:** Varies
**INSTRUCTION FORM:** Yes

**ACKNOWLEDGED:** Yes
**REVIEW PROCESS:** External reviewers
**NOTIFICATION TIME:** 1-6 months

**CRITICISM:** Yes

**ACCEPTANCE RATE:** Varies
**REVISION:** Medium
**EARLY PUBLICATION OPTION:** No
**COPYRIGHT POLICY:** Publisher
**FEE:** None
**REPRINTS:** 100 if page charges honored
**PUBLICATION TIME LAG:** 12 months
**PROOFS:** Yes
**PAGE CHARGES:** $70 per printed page

**JOURNAL TITLE:** IEEE Transactions on Professional Communication

**SUBSCRIPTION ADDRESS:** IEEE Service Center, 445 Hoes Lane, Piscataway, NJ 08854

**PRICE:** $32
**FREQUENCY:** Quarterly
**CIRCULATION:** 3,000
**AFFILIATION:** Institute of Electrical and Electronics Engineers
**INDEXED/ABSTRACTED:** EnI

**MANUSCRIPT ADDRESS:** R. J. Joenk, IBM Corporation, P.O. Box 1900, Boulder, CO 80302

**EDITORIAL POLICY:** Help engineers and others who need to be technical communicators improve their skills and to present new ideas and methods in communication

**AUDIENCE:** Practicing engineers and scientists, technical managers, writers, editors, and teachers

**PREFERRED TOPICS:** Pragmatic discussions, tutorials, and "how to" treatments of communication problems

**INAPPROPRIATE TOPICS:** Not given

**FEATURES:** Not given

**REVIEWS:** Yes
**STUDENT PAPERS:** No

**RESTRICTIONS:** None
**COVER LETTER:** Yes
**NUMBER OF COPIES:** 2
**STYLE:** House
**FORMAT:** Standard
**ABSTRACT:** 100-200
**LENGTH:** 3,000
**INSTRUCTION FORM:** Yes

**ACKNOWLEDGED:** Yes
**REVIEW PROCESS:** Not given
**NOTIFICATION TIME:** 4-8 weeks

**CRITICISM:** Yes

**ACCEPTANCE RATE:** 60%
**REVISION:** Medium
**EARLY PUBLICATION OPTION:** No
**COPYRIGHT POLICY:** Publisher
**FEE:** None
**REPRINTS:** None; may be purchased in multiples of 100
**PUBLICATION TIME LAG:** 4 months
**PROOFS:** Yes
**PAGE CHARGES:** No

**JOURNAL TITLE:** IFLA Journal

**SUBSCRIPTION ADDRESS:** K. G. Saur Verlag, KG, POB 7110 09, Pösstenbacherstrasse 2b, D8000, München 71, West Germany

**PRICE:** DM58
**CIRCULATION:** 1,800
**AFFILIATION:** International Federation of Library Associations and Institutions
**INDEXED/ABSTRACTED:** ISA, LISA, LL
**FREQUENCY:** Quarterly

**MANUSCRIPT ADDRESS:** Committee's Secretary, c/o IFLA, Netherlands Congress Building, Churchillplein 10, P.O.B. 82128, NL-2508EC, The Hague, Netherlands

**EDITORIAL POLICY:** The official organ of IFLA. In addition to state-of-the-art articles and reports of research in progress, association news is covered prominently.

**AUDIENCE:** All librarians

**PREFERRED TOPICS:** Case studies, review articles, commentaries

**INAPPROPRIATE TOPICS:** Articles limited to progress in one country that cannot be extrapolated to other countries; articles of a too technical nature

**FEATURES:** IFLA activities, reports on meetings attended by IFLA representatives

**REVIEWS:** No                **STUDENT PAPERS:** No

**RESTRICTIONS:** No
**COVER LETTER:** Yes
**NUMBER OF COPIES:** 1
**STYLE:** Not given
**FORMAT:** Standard
**ABSTRACT:** 100
**LENGTH:** 9-12 pages
**INSTRUCTION FORM:** Yes

**ACKNOWLEDGED:** Yes
**REVIEW PROCESS:** Editorial board
**NOTIFICATION TIME:** 2 months

**CRITICISM:** Yes

**ACCEPTANCE RATE:** 60-70%
**REVISION:** Medium
**EARLY PUBLICATION OPTION:** No
**COPYRIGHT POLICY:** Not given
**FEE:** None
**REPRINTS:** 3 copies of issue
**PUBLICATION TIME LAG:** 6 months
**PROOFS:** No
**PAGE CHARGES:** No

**JOURNAL TITLE:** IMC Journal

**SUBSCRIPTION ADDRESS:** IMC Journal, 100 East 14th Street, Minneapolis, MN 55403

**PRICE:** $20
**CIRCULATION:** 20,000
**AFFILIATION:** International Micrographic Congress
**INDEXED/ABSTRACTED:** Not given
**FREQUENCY:** Quarterly

**MANUSCRIPT ADDRESS:** Karen Morrison, IMC Journal, P.O. Box 22440, San Diego, CA 92122

**EDITORIAL POLICY:** A journal devoted to all aspects of micrographics and applications

**AUDIENCE:** Anyone, newcomers and professionals in the field of microforms
**PREFERRED TOPICS:** International news and microfilm use

**INAPPROPRIATE TOPICS:** Non-microfilm press releases

**FEATURES:** Micrographic forum

**REVIEWS:** Yes
**STUDENT PAPERS:** Not given

**RESTRICTIONS:** None
**COVER LETTER:** Yes
**NUMBER OF COPIES:** 1
**STYLE:** Any acceptable
**FORMAT:** Any acceptable
**ABSTRACT:** No
**LENGTH:** Not given
**INSTRUCTION FORM:** No

**ACKNOWLEDGED:** Yes
**REVIEW PROCESS:** Editorial board
**NOTIFICATION TIME:** Not given

**CRITICISM:** Yes

**ACCEPTANCE RATE:** Not given
**REVISION:** Light
**EARLY PUBLICATION OPTION:** No
**COPYRIGHT POLICY:** Publisher
**FEE:** None
**REPRINTS:** Reasonable number of copies of issue
**PUBLICATION TIME LAG:** 3 months
**PROOFS:** Yes
**PAGE CHARGES:** No

JOURNAL TITLE: Indexer

SUBSCRIPTION ADDRESS: The Treasurer, 26 Golders Rise, London NW4 2HR, England

PRICE: $11.40
CIRCULATION: 1,800
AFFILIATION: The Society of Indexers
INDEXED/ABSTRACTED: AI, CA, INSPEC, ISA, LISA, LL

FREQUENCY: Biannual

MANUSCRIPT ADDRESS: Hazel K. Bell, 139 The Ryde, Hatsfield, Herts AL9 5DP England

EDITORIAL POLICY: Articles on compiling and using indexes, including typographical presentation, and reviews of similar material, including published indexes

AUDIENCE: Indexers and authors, publishing houses, universities and other academic institutions, and libraries

PREFERRED TOPICS: Articles concerning indexes or the compiling of indexes

INAPPROPRIATE TOPICS: Not given

FEATURES: Extracts from published book reviews which mention indexes

REVIEWS: Yes
STUDENT PAPERS: No

RESTRICTIONS: No
COVER LETTER: Yes
NUMBER OF COPIES: 2
STYLE: Collins
FORMAT: Standard

ABSTRACT: 150
LENGTH: Varies
INSTRUCTION FORM: Yes

ACKNOWLEDGED: Yes
REVIEW PROCESS: Editorial board and external reviewers

NOTIFICATION TIME: 2-3 weeks

CRITICISM: No

ACCEPTANCE RATE: 80%
REVISION: Light
EARLY PUBLICATION OPTION: No
COPYRIGHT POLICY: Author
FEE: None
REPRINTS: 6-10

PUBLICATION TIME LAG: 6-12 months
PROOFS: Only if resident of England
PAGE CHARGES: No

JOURNAL TITLE: Information Hotline

SUBSCRIPTION ADDRESS: Science Associates, P.O. Box 196, Marlboro, NJ 07746

PRICE: $50
CIRCULATION: Not given
AFFILIATION: None
INDEXED/ABSTRACTED: CIS, ISA, LL, LISA

FREQUENCY: Monthly

MANUSCRIPT ADDRESS: Marilyn G. McCormick, Science Associates/International, Inc., 1841 Broadway, New York, NY 10023

EDITORIAL POLICY: Objective and comprehensive data base news

AUDIENCE: Librarians, computer control heads, information managers

PREFERRED TOPICS: News of data bases, networks, information economics

INAPPROPRIATE TOPICS: Not given

FEATURES: Specialized bibliographies and glossaries, opinions of trends

REVIEWS: Yes

STUDENT PAPERS: No

RESTRICTIONS: Requested articles only
COVER LETTER: N/A
NUMBER OF COPIES: 1
STYLE: No recommendation
FORMAT: No recommendation

ABSTRACT: No
LENGTH: Varies
INSTRUCTION FORM: No

ACKNOWLEDGED: Yes
REVIEW PROCESS: Editorial board and external reviewers
CRITICISM: No

NOTIFICATION TIME: 4 weeks

ACCEPTANCE RATE: 100%
REVISION: Medium
EARLY PUBLICATION OPTION: No
COPYRIGHT POLICY: Flexible
FEE: None
REPRINTS: Negotiable

PUBLICATION TIME LAG: 2-6 months
PROOFS: Yes
PAGE CHARGES: No

JOURNAL TITLE: Information Retrieval & Library Automation

SUBSCRIPTION ADDRESS: Lomond Publications, P.O. Box 56, Mt. Airy, MD 21771

PRICE: $36
CIRCULATION: 1,500
AFFILIATION: None
INDEXED/ABSTRACTED: Not given

FREQUENCY: Monthly

MANUSCRIPT ADDRESS: Lowell H. Hattery, P.O. Box 56, Mt. Airy, MD 21771

EDITORIAL POLICY: News stories, editorials, and literature reviews related to innovation in the handling, storage, retrieval, transfer and utilization of information

AUDIENCE: Information specialists, information managers, librarians, researchers

PREFERRED TOPICS: New developments, research findings

INAPPROPRIATE TOPICS: Not given

FEATURES: Not given

REVIEWS: Yes

STUDENT PAPERS: Yes

RESTRICTIONS: None
COVER LETTER: Yes
NUMBER OF COPIES: 1
STYLE: No requirements
FORMAT: No requirements

ABSTRACT: No
LENGTH: 500-1,000
INSTRUCTION FORM: No

ACKNOWLEDGED: Yes
REVIEW PROCESS: Editor

NOTIFICATION TIME: 30 days

CRITICISM: No

ACCEPTANCE RATE: Not given
REVISION: Not given
EARLY PUBLICATION OPTION: No
COPYRIGHT POLICY: Publisher
FEE: $25
REPRINTS: 10

PUBLICATION TIME LAG: 30-60 days
PROOFS: Not given

PAGE CHARGES: No

**JOURNAL TITLE:** Instructional Innovator

**SUBSCRIPTION ADDRESS:** Circulation Department, AECT, 1126 16th St., N.W., Washington, DC 20036

**PRICE:** $18
**CIRCULATION:** 16,000
**AFFILIATION:** Association for Educational Communications and Technology
**INDEXED/ABSTRACTED:** Media Review Digest, CC, CIJE, ECER, EdI, IIMMI, INSPEC, MRS

**FREQUENCY:** 9 x a year

**MANUSCRIPT ADDRESS:** Howard Hitchens, AECT, 1126 16th St., N.W., Washington, DC 22036

**EDITORIAL POLICY:** Written for those instructional professionals who are the leaders in the adaptation of technological advances to the learning process

**AUDIENCE:** Anyone involved in using technology to help people learn better

**PREFERRED TOPICS:** Case studies, theoretical or historical topics, how-to ideas--must be useful to instructors in a wide variety of traditional and nontraditional instructional settings

**INAPPROPRIATE TOPICS:** Articles from people who have just "discovered" elementary technology in the classroom

**FEATURES:** Each issue has a special theme; feature articles related to the theme are solicited

**REVIEWS:** No

**STUDENT PAPERS:** No

**RESTRICTIONS:** None
**COVER LETTER:** Not necessary
**NUMBER OF COPIES:** 2
**STYLE:** House
**FORMAT:** Standard

**ABSTRACT:** No
**LENGTH:** 1,500
**INSTRUCTION FORM:** Yes

**ACKNOWLEDGED:** Yes
**REVIEW PROCESS:** Not given

**NOTIFICATION TIME:** 3-4 months

**CRITICISM:** No

**ACCEPTANCE RATE:** 25%
**REVISION:** Medium
**EARLY PUBLICATION OPTION:** No
**COPYRIGHT POLICY:** Publisher preferably
**FEE:** None
**REPRINTS:** None

**PUBLICATION TIME LAG:** 6-8 weeks
**PROOFS:** Yes
**PAGE CHARGES:** No

**JOURNAL TITLE:** International Association of Agricultural Librarians and Documentalists Quarterly Bulletin
**SUBSCRIPTION ADDRESS:** Quarterly Bulletin of IAALD, The Secretary/Treasurer, Central Veterinary Lab, New Haw, Weybridge, Surrey KT15 3NB England

**PRICE:** $12
**FREQUENCY:** Quarterly
**CIRCULATION:** 550
**AFFILIATION:** International Association of Ag. Libns. & Docs.
**INDEXED/ABSTRACTED:** LL, LISA

**MANUSCRIPT ADDRESS:** Richard Farley, Quarterly Bulletin of the International Association of Agricultural Librarians and Documentalists, National Agricultural Library, Beltsville, MD 20705
**EDITORIAL POLICY:** Not given

**AUDIENCE:** Agricultural librarians and documentalists

**PREFERRED TOPICS:** Material concerned with agricultural information

**INAPPROPRIATE TOPICS:** Not given

**FEATURES:** Not given

**REVIEWS:** Yes
**STUDENT PAPERS:** No

**RESTRICTIONS:** No
**COVER LETTER:** Yes
**NUMBER OF COPIES:** 1
**STYLE:** Chicago
**FORMAT:** Standard
**ABSTRACT:** 50
**LENGTH:** 6,000
**INSTRUCTION FORM:** Yes

**ACKNOWLEDGED:** If desired
**NOTIFICATION TIME:** 1 month
**REVIEW PROCESS:** Reviewed by two editors

**CRITICISM:** Sometimes

**ACCEPTANCE RATE:** 70%
**PUBLICATION TIME LAG:** 6 months
**REVISION:** Medium
**PROOFS:** Yes
**EARLY PUBLICATION OPTION:** No
**PAGE CHARGES:** No
**COPYRIGHT POLICY:** Publisher
**FEE:** None
**REPRINTS:** 1 copy of issue

JOURNAL TITLE: International Cataloguing

SUBSCRIPTION ADDRESS: Journals Division, Longmans Group, Ltd. 43/45 Annandale Street, Edinburgh EH7 4AT, UK

PRICE: $15
CIRCULATION: 900
AFFILIATION: IFLA International Office for UBC
INDEXED/ABSTRACTED: LISA, LL

FREQUENCY: Quarterly

MANUSCRIPT ADDRESS: Mrs. D. Anderson, Director, IFLA International Office for UBC, c/o Reference Division, British Library, Great Russell St., London WC1B 3DG, England
EDITORIAL POLICY: One article in each issue dealing with a particular cataloging problem; the remainder made up of news about cataloging activities throughout the world
AUDIENCE: The library community and the abstracting and indexing community
PREFERRED TOPICS: Cataloging activities throughout the world

INAPPROPRIATE TOPICS: Not given

FEATURES: One article in each issue deals with a particular cataloging problem

REVIEWS: Yes
STUDENT PAPERS: No

RESTRICTIONS: None
COVER LETTER: Yes
NUMBER OF COPIES: 2
STYLE: Not given
FORMAT: Standard

ABSTRACT: No
LENGTH: 3,000-6,000
INSTRUCTION FORM: No

ACKNOWLEDGED: Yes
REVIEW PROCESS: Not given

NOTIFICATION TIME: 2 weeks

CRITICISM: No

ACCEPTANCE RATE: 80%
REVISION: Heavy
EARLY PUBLICATION OPTION: No
COPYRIGHT POLICY: Not copyrighted
FEE: None
REPRINTS: 3 copies of issue

PUBLICATION TIME LAG: 1-6 months
PROOFS: No
PAGE CHARGES: No

**JOURNAL TITLE:** International Classification
**SUBSCRIPTION ADDRESS:** K. G. Saur Publishing, 175 Fifth Avenue, New York, NY 10010

**PRICE:** $26
**CIRCULATION:** 500
**AFFILIATION:** FID/CR; IFLA International Office for UBC; Gessell-
**INDEXED/ABSTRACTED:** BSI01, LISA, LL, RZ    schaft für Klassification Ev
**FREQUENCY:** 3 x a year

**MANUSCRIPT ADDRESS:** J. Dahlberg, Soogstrasse 36a, D-6000 Frankfurt 50, West Germany

**EDITORIAL POLICY:** Devoted to concept theory, organization of knowledge and data, and systematic terminology

**AUDIENCE:** Librarians, information scientists, anybody else interested in classification
**PREFERRED TOPICS:** Original articles, reports about conferences

**INAPPROPRIATE TOPICS:** Not given

**FEATURES:** Bibliographic section called classification literature, and detailed book reviews

**REVIEWS:** Yes
**STUDENT PAPERS:** No

**RESTRICTIONS:** None
**COVER LETTER:** Yes
**NUMBER OF COPIES:** 2
**STYLE:** House
**FORMAT:** Standard
**ABSTRACT:** 100-200
**LENGTH:** 1,500-3,000
**INSTRUCTION FORM:** Yes

**ACKNOWLEDGED:** Yes
**REVIEW PROCESS:** Editorial board and external reviewers
**NOTIFICATION TIME:** 4-8 weeks

**CRITICISM:** Yes

**ACCEPTANCE RATE:** 70%
**REVISION:** Varies
**EARLY PUBLICATION OPTION:** No
**COPYRIGHT POLICY:** Publisher
**FEE:** None
**REPRINTS:** 25
**PUBLICATION TIME LAG:** 6 months
**PROOFS:** Yes
**PAGE CHARGES:** No

JOURNAL TITLE: International Forum on Information and Documentation
SUBSCRIPTION ADDRESS: FID, P.O. Box 30115, 2500GC The Hague, Netherlands

PRICE: $30
CIRCULATION: 800
AFFILIATION: International Federation for Documentation
INDEXED/ABSTRACTED: ISA, LISA, SSCI
FREQUENCY: Quarterly

MANUSCRIPT ADDRESS: A.I. Mikhailov, VINITI, Baltijskaya ul. 14, 125219, Moscow, USSR

EDITORIAL POLICY: Intended to cover the most important problems of information theory and practical activities which are of interest to information specialists
AUDIENCE: Information specialists, editors and publishers
PREFERRED TOPICS: Communication in science, conventional and advanced forms and ways of information presentation and dissemination, forecasting and planning of development trends
INAPPROPRIATE TOPICS: Not given

FEATURES: Special issues on particular topics when necessary

REVIEWS: Yes
STUDENT PAPERS: No

RESTRICTIONS: None
COVER LETTER: Yes
NUMBER OF COPIES: 2
STYLE: House
FORMAT: Standard
ABSTRACT: 250
LENGTH: 5,000
INSTRUCTION FORM: Yes

ACKNOWLEDGED: Yes
REVIEW PROCESS: Editorial board or external reviewers
NOTIFICATION TIME: 1 month

CRITICISM: Yes

ACCEPTANCE RATE: 90%
REVISION: Varies
EARLY PUBLICATION OPTION: No
COPYRIGHT POLICY: Publisher
FEE: None
REPRINTS: 10
PUBLICATION TIME LAG: 6 months
PROOFS: Seldom
PAGE CHARGES: No

JOURNAL TITLE: Journal of Academic Librarianship

SUBSCRIPTION ADDRESS: Mountainside Publishing, P.O. Box 8330, Ann Arbor, MI 48107

PRICE: $16
CIRCULATION: 3,000
AFFILIATION: None
INDEXED/ABSTRACTED: BRI, CALL, LISA, LL, SSCI
FREQUENCY: Bimonthly

MANUSCRIPT ADDRESS: Richard M. Dougherty, P.O. Box 8330, Ann Arbor, MI 48107

EDITORIAL POLICY: Provides academic librarians and other practitioners with results of research findings in the field, addresses the current issues confronting the profession
AUDIENCE: Library practitioners in general; academic librarians in particular
PREFERRED TOPICS: Those related to academic librarianship

INAPPROPRIATE TOPICS: Library instruction articles; "how-we-did-it-good" pieces

FEATURES: Symposia, photo essays

REVIEWS:
STUDENT PAPERS: Yes

RESTRICTIONS: None
COVER LETTER: Yes
NUMBER OF COPIES: 2
STYLE: Chicago
FORMAT: Standard
ABSTRACT: 100
LENGTH: 2,000-5,000
INSTRUCTION FORM: Yes

ACKNOWLEDGED: Yes
REVIEW PROCESS: Editorial board; external reviewers when necessary
CRITICISM: Yes
NOTIFICATION TIME: 4-6 weeks

ACCEPTANCE RATE: 15-20%
REVISION: Medium
EARLY PUBLICATION OPTION: No
COPYRIGHT POLICY: Publisher
FEE: $25-$50 at time of publication
REPRINTS: 6 copies of issue
PUBLICATION TIME LAG: 6-12 months
PROOFS: Yes
PAGE CHARGES: No

**JOURNAL TITLE:** Journal of Chemical Information and Computer Sciences

**SUBSCRIPTION ADDRESS:** American Chemical Society, 1155 16th St., N.W., Washington, DC 20036

**PRICE:** $44
**CIRCULATION:** 2,200
**AFFILIATION:** American Chemical Society
**INDEXED/ABSTRACTED:** CA

**FREQUENCY:** Quarterly

**MANUSCRIPT ADDRESS:** Herman Skolnik, American Chemical Society, 1155 16th St., N.W., Washington, DC 20036

**EDITORIAL POLICY:** The journal invites previously unpublished and original contributions

**AUDIENCE:** Information and computer scientists, librarians and chemists

**PREFERRED TOPICS:** New and original material resulting from research and development, significant review papers and those describing new operations and services

**INAPPROPRIATE TOPICS:** Sales promotions and pape-s which treat an old subject as something new

**FEATURES:** Award addresses and unique talks relative to chemical information and computer science

**REVIEWS:** Yes

**STUDENT PAPERS:** No

**RESTRICTIONS:** None
**COVER LETTER:** Yes
**NUMBER OF COPIES:** 3
**STYLE:** House
**FORMAT:** Standard

**ABSTRACT:** 100
**LENGTH:** 5,000-6,000
**INSTRUCTION FORM:** Yes

**ACKNOWLEDGED:** Yes
**REVIEW PROCESS:** External reviewers

**NOTIFICATION TIME:** 3 months

**CRITICISM:** Yes

**ACCEPTANCE RATE:** 65%
**REVISION:** Medium
**EARLY PUBLICATION OPTION:** No
**COPYRIGHT POLICY:** Publisher
**FEE:** None
**REPRINTS:** None free; may be purchased

**PUBLICATION TIME LAG:** 3-6 months
**PROOFS:** Yes

**PAGE CHARGES:** $40 per printed page

**JOURNAL TITLE:** Journal of Computer and Information Sciences

**SUBSCRIPTION ADDRESS:** Plenum Publishing Corp., 227 West 17th St., New York, NY 10011

**PRICE:** $98
**CIRCULATION:** 4,000
**AFFILIATION:** None
**INDEXED/ABSTRACTED:** Not given

**FREQUENCY:** Bimonthly

**MANUSCRIPT ADDRESS:** Julius T. Tou, Center for Informatics Research, University of Florida, Gainesville, FL 32601

**EDITORIAL POLICY:** Research papers and tutorial-type surveys which take in software engineering; systems programming, pattern recognition; computer graphics; information retrieval, automata theory; linguistics, etc.
**AUDIENCE:** Researchers with interest in computer and information science
**PREFERRED TOPICS:** Research papers, survey of recent developments, tutorial and expository papers

**INAPPROPRIATE TOPICS:** Not given

**FEATURES:** Tutorial

**REVIEWS:** Not given

**STUDENT PAPERS:** Yes

**RESTRICTIONS:** None
**COVER LETTER:** Yes
**NUMBER OF COPIES:** 3
**STYLE:** See journal
**FORMAT:** Standard

**ABSTRACT:** 150
**LENGTH:** Varies
**INSTRUCTION FORM:** Yes

**ACKNOWLEDGED:** Yes
**REVIEW PROCESS:** Editor and external reviewers

**NOTIFICATION TIME:** 3 months

**CRITICISM:** Yes

**ACCEPTANCE RATE:** 50%
**REVISION:** Light
**EARLY PUBLICATION OPTION:** Not given
**COPYRIGHT POLICY:** Publisher
**FEE:** None
**REPRINTS:** None

**PUBLICATION TIME LAG:** 3 months
**PROOFS:** Yes

**PAGE CHARGES:** No

JOURNAL TITLE: Journal of Cybernetics

SUBSCRIPTION ADDRESS: Hemisphere Publishing Corp., 1025 Vermont Ave., N.W., Washington, DC 20005

PRICE: $85
CIRCULATION: 350
AFFILIATION: Austrian Society for Cybernetic Studies
INDEXED/ABSTRACTED: BA, CC

FREQUENCY: Quarterly

MANUSCRIPT ADDRESS: Robert Trappl, Department of Medical Cybernetics, University of Vienna Medical School, Freyung 6, A-1010, Vienna, Austria

EDITORIAL POLICY: To disseminate information to the scientific community on important methodological developments in cybernetics at a formal level

AUDIENCE: Scientists and others involved in the field of cybernetics

PREFERRED TOPICS: Systems research; organization; information sciences; stochastic programming; modeling; management systems

INAPPROPRIATE TOPICS: Detailed methematical papers; fuzzy sets

FEATURES: International Cybernetics Newsletter

REVIEWS: Yes
STUDENT PAPERS: No

RESTRICTIONS: None
COVER LETTER: Yes
NUMBER OF COPIES: 2
STYLE: House
FORMAT: Standard

ABSTRACT: 50-100
LENGTH: 3,000-4,000
INSTRUCTION FORM: Yes

ACKNOWLEDGED: Yes
REVIEW PROCESS: Editorial board and external reviewers

NOTIFICATION TIME: 3-6 months

CRITICISM: Yes

ACCEPTANCE RATE: 70%
REVISION: Light
EARLY PUBLICATION OPTION: No
COPYRIGHT POLICY: Publisher
FEE: None
REPRINTS: 20

PUBLICATION TIME LAG: 6-9 months
PROOFS: Yes
PAGE CHARGES: No

**JOURNAL TITLE:** Journal of Documentation

**SUBSCRIPTION ADDRESS:** Aslib, Subscriptions Department, 3 Belgrave Square, London, SW1X 8PL, UK

**PRICE:** $37
**CIRCULATION:** 3,300
**AFFILIATION:** Aslib
**INDEXED/ABSTRACTED:** CA, CC, ISA, LISA, LL

**FREQUENCY:** Quarterly

**MANUSCRIPT ADDRESS:** Karen Sparck Jones, Aslib, 3 Belgrave Square, London SW1X 8PL, UK

**EDITORIAL POLICY:** Articles deal with methods of presenting information, including translations, abstracts, indexes and other bibliographic aids

**AUDIENCE:** Scholars and librarians, information scientists

**PREFERRED TOPICS:** Articles dealing with the recording, organization, and classification and dissemination of information

**INAPPROPRIATE TOPICS:** Papers using mathematical methods because of their mathematical interest

**FEATURES:** Progress in documentation

**REVIEWS:** Yes
**STUDENT PAPERS:** No

**RESTRICTIONS:** None
**COVER LETTER:** Yes
**NUMBER OF COPIES:** 2
**STYLE:** Burbidge
**FORMAT:** Standard
**ABSTRACT:** 200
**LENGTH:** 4,000-5,000
**INSTRUCTION FORM:** No; see journal

**ACKNOWLEDGED:** Yes
**REVIEW PROCESS:** Editorial board and external reviewers
**NOTIFICATION TIME:** Varies

**CRITICISM:** Summarily

**ACCEPTANCE RATE:** Less than 40%
**REVISION:** Light
**EARLY PUBLICATION OPTION:** No
**COPYRIGHT POLICY:** Publisher and author
**FEE:** Expenses only, on publication
**REPRINTS:** 25
**PUBLICATION TIME LAG:** up to 6 months
**PROOFS:** Yes
**PAGE CHARGES:** No

**JOURNAL TITLE:** Journal of Education for Librarianship

**SUBSCRIPTION ADDRESS:** Journal of Education for Librarianship, Association of American Library Schools, 471 Park Lane, State College, PA 61801

**PRICE:** $12
**CIRCULATION:** 5,000
**AFFILIATION:** Association of American Library Schools
**INDEXED/ABSTRACTED:** EdI, LISA, LL
**FREQUENCY:** Quarterly

**MANUSCRIPT ADDRESS:** Charles Patterson, Library School, Louisiana State University, Baton Rouge, LA 70803

**EDITORIAL POLICY:** A scholarly journal in the field of library and information science education; serves as forum for discussion and presentation of research in the field

**AUDIENCE:** Library and information science educators

**PREFERRED TOPICS:** Those related to the education of librarians and information scientists

**INAPPROPRIATE TOPICS:** Manuscripts pertaining to instruction in the use of libraries

**FEATURES:** Annual salary survey of library school faculty; editorial collumns on research, teaching methods, and continuing education for librarians

**REVIEWS:** No
**STUDENT PAPERS:** No

**RESTRICTIONS:** None
**COVER LETTER:** Yes
**NUMBER OF COPIES:** 3
**STYLE:** Chicago
**FORMAT:** Standard
**ABSTRACT:** 150
**LENGTH:** 2,000-3,000
**INSTRUCTION FORM:** Yes

**ACKNOWLEDGED:** Yes
**REVIEW PROCESS:** Editorial board and external reviewers
**NOTIFICATION TIME:** 6-9 months

**CRITICISM:** When applicable

**ACCEPTANCE RATE:** 8%
**REVISION:** Varies
**EARLY PUBLICATION OPTION:** No
**COPYRIGHT POLICY:** Publisher
**FEE:** None
**REPRINTS:** None
**PUBLICATION TIME LAG:** 6 months
**PROOFS:** Yes
**PAGE CHARGES:** No

JOURNAL TITLE: Journal of Librarianship

SUBSCRIPTION ADDRESS: Sales Department, Library Association, 7 Ridgmount St., London WC1E 7AE England

PRICE: $32
CIRCULATION: 1,500
AFFILIATION: Library Association
INDEXED/ABSTRACTED: LISA

FREQUENCY: Quarterly

MANUSCRIPT ADDRESS: Editor, Journal of Librarianship, Library Association, 7 Ridgmount Street, London WC1E 7AE England

EDITORIAL POLICY: Deals with all aspects of library and information work in the UK and abroad

AUDIENCE: Librarians

PREFERRED TOPICS: Results of research and investigation into library and information work

INAPPROPRIATE TOPICS: Not given

FEATURES: None

REVIEWS: Yes, commissioned    STUDENT PAPERS: No

RESTRICTIONS: No
COVER LETTER: Yes
NUMBER OF COPIES: 2
STYLE: House
FORMAT: Standard

ABSTRACT: 50-60
LENGTH: 6,000-7,000
INSTRUCTION FORM: Yes

ACKNOWLEDGED: Yes
REVIEW PROCESS: Editorial board and external reviewers

NOTIFICATION TIME: 4 months

CRITICISM: No

ACCEPTANCE RATE: 30%
REVISION: Light
EARLY PUBLICATION OPTION: No
COPYRIGHT POLICY: Author
FEE: $50 on publication
REPRINTS: None

PUBLICATION TIME LAG: 7 months
PROOFS: Yes
PAGE CHARGES: No

**JOURNAL TITLE:** Journal of Library Administration

**SUBSCRIPTION ADDRESS:** Haworth Press, 28 East 22 Street, New York, NY 10010

**PRICE:** $48
**CIRCULATION:** Not given (new journal)
**AFFILIATION:** None
**INDEXED/ABSTRACTED:** Not yet

**FREQUENCY:** Quarterly

**MANUSCRIPT ADDRESS:** Dr. John R. Rizzo, Ed. Department of Management, Western Michigan University, Kalamazoo, MI 49001

**EDITORIAL POLICY:** Devoted to advancing management theory and application in library and information service organizations and systems

**AUDIENCE:** Library administrators/students in all spheres

**PREFERRED TOPICS:** Original pieces (theory, practice) on any topic in management

**INAPPROPRIATE TOPICS:** Articles on "local" narrow cases with little interpretation and/or generalizing

**FEATURES:** Book reviews, special features on particular management topics, accountability, training, etc.

**REVIEWS:** Yes

**STUDENT PAPERS:** No

**RESTRICTIONS:** None
**COVER LETTER:** Yes
**NUMBER OF COPIES:** 3
**STYLE:** Chicago or APA
**FORMAT:** Standard

**ABSTRACT:** No
**LENGTH:** Varies
**INSTRUCTION FORM:** Yes

**ACKNOWLEDGED:** Yes
**REVIEW PROCESS:** Editorial board and external reviewers

**NOTIFICATION TIME:** 2 months

**CRITICISM:** Yes

**ACCEPTANCE RATE:** Unknown
**REVISION:** Medium
**EARLY PUBLICATION OPTION:** Yes
**COPYRIGHT POLICY:** Publisher
**FEE:** None
**REPRINTS:** 10

**PUBLICATION TIME LAG:** 9-12 months
**PROOFS:** Yes
**PAGE CHARGES:** No

JOURNAL TITLE: Journal of Library and Information Science

SUBSCRIPTION ADDRESS: Chinese Culture Service, Inc., P.O. Box 444, Oak Park, IL 60603

PRICE: $10
CIRCULATION: 800
AFFILIATION: Chinese American Librarians Association
INDEXED/ABSTRACTED: ICP, ISA, LISA, LL, PAIS

FREQUENCY: Semiannual

MANUSCRIPT ADDRESS: Prof. Tze-Chung Li, Rosary College, Graduate School of Library Science, River Forest, IL 60305

EDITORIAL POLICY: A forum for librarians and information scientists in Taiwan and abroad to discuss problems common to their work

AUDIENCE: Professional librarians

PREFERRED TOPICS: See editorial policy above

INAPPROPRIATE TOPICS: Not given

FEATURES: Proceedings of the Chinese American Librarians Association

REVIEWS: Yes                    STUDENT PAPERS: Yes

RESTRICTIONS: None
COVER LETTER: No
NUMBER OF COPIES: 2
STYLE: House
FORMAT: Standard

ABSTRACT: 200
LENGTH: 5,000-10,000
INSTRUCTION FORM: Yes

ACKNOWLEDGED: Yes
REVIEW PROCESS: Editorial board and external reviewers

NOTIFICATION TIME: 10 days

CRITICISM: Occasionally

ACCEPTANCE RATE: 70%
REVISION: Medium
EARLY PUBLICATION OPTION: No
COPYRIGHT POLICY: Publisher
FEE: None
REPRINTS: 30

PUBLICATION TIME LAG: 3-6 months
PROOFS: Yes

PAGE CHARGES: No

JOURNAL TITLE: Journal of Library Automation

SUBSCRIPTION ADDRESS: American Library Association, 50 E. Huron St., Chicago, IL 60611

PRICE: $15
CIRCULATION: 5,500
AFFILIATION: American Library Association
INDEXED/ABSTRACTED: CC, CIJE, CIS, CR, INSPEC, ISA, LISA, LL, QBCDP

FREQUENCY: Quarterly

MANUSCRIPT ADDRESS: Susan K. Martin, Milton D. Eisenhower Library, Johns Hopkins University, Baltimore, MD 21218

EDITORIAL POLICY: Research and development in library automation, the history and teaching of information science, systems and designs in libraries

AUDIENCE: Librarians and library automation educators

PREFERRED TOPICS: Automation, videocable, audio-visual services

INAPPROPRIATE TOPICS: Not given

FEATURES: Technical communications

REVIEWS: Yes                STUDENT PAPERS: No

RESTRICTIONS: None
COVER LETTER: Yes
NUMBER OF COPIES: 2
STYLE: Chicago
FORMAT: Standard

ABSTRACT: 100
LENGTH: 15 pages
INSTRUCTION FORM: No, see journal

ACKNOWLEDGED: Yes
REVIEW PROCESS: Editorial board

NOTIFICATION TIME: 8 weeks

CRITICISM: Yes

ACCEPTANCE RATE: 65%
REVISION: Varies
EARLY PUBLICATION OPTION: No
COPYRIGHT POLICY: Publisher
FEE: None
REPRINTS: None

PUBLICATION TIME LAG: 6-8 months
PROOFS: Yes
PAGE CHARGES: No

| | |
|---|---|
| **JOURNAL TITLE:** | Journal of Library History |
| **SUBSCRIPTION ADDRESS:** | Journal of Library History, University of Texas Press, Box 7819, Austin, TX 78712 |

| | | | |
|---|---|---|---|
| **PRICE:** | $15 | **FREQUENCY:** | Quarterly |
| **CIRCULATION:** | 1,100 | | |
| **AFFILIATION:** | None | | |
| **INDEXED/ABSTRACTED:** | BBF, BRI, CALL, HA, LISA, LL, SSCI | | |

| | |
|---|---|
| **MANUSCRIPT ADDRESS:** | Donald G. Davis, Jr., Journal of Library History, Graduate School of Library Science, The University of Texas, Box 7576, Austin, TX 78712 |
| **EDITORIAL POLICY:** | Examines and explicates the role of libraries in society |
| **AUDIENCE:** | Historians, library educators |
| **PREFERRED TOPICS:** | Articles on library history, philosophy, comparative librarianship |
| **INAPPROPRIATE TOPICS:** | Anecdotal treatment of a single library, collection, or librarian |
| **FEATURES:** | Not given |

| | | | |
|---|---|---|---|
| **REVIEWS:** | Yes | **STUDENT PAPERS:** | No |

| | | | |
|---|---|---|---|
| **RESTRICTIONS:** | None | | |
| **COVER LETTER:** | Yes | | |
| **NUMBER OF COPIES:** | 2 | **ABSTRACT:** | 150 |
| **STYLE:** | Chicago | **LENGTH:** | 5,000-6,000 |
| **FORMAT:** | Standard | **INSTRUCTION FORM:** | Yes |

| | | | |
|---|---|---|---|
| **ACKNOWLEDGED:** | Yes | **NOTIFICATION TIME:** | 3 months |
| **REVIEW PROCESS:** | Editorial board and external reviewers | | |
| **CRITICISM:** | Yes | | |

| | | | |
|---|---|---|---|
| **ACCEPTANCE RATE:** | 55% | **PUBLICATION TIME LAG:** | 6-12 months |
| **REVISION:** | Medium | **PROOFS:** | No |
| **EARLY PUBLICATION OPTION:** | No | **PAGE CHARGES:** | No |
| **COPYRIGHT POLICY:** | Publisher | | |
| **FEE:** | None | | |
| **REPRINTS:** | 2 copies of issue; reprints may be purchased | | |

**JOURNAL TITLE:** Journal of Micrographics

**SUBSCRIPTION ADDRESS:** National Micrographics Association, 8719 Colesville Road, Silver Spring, MD 20910

**PRICE:** $35
**CIRCULATION:** 10,000
**AFFILIATION:** National Micrographics Association
**INDEXED/ABSTRACTED:** Not given
**FREQUENCY:** Bimonthly

**MANUSCRIPT ADDRESS:** Ellen T. Meyer, 8719 Colesville Road, Silver Spring, MD 20910

**EDITORIAL POLICY:** To publish original work pertaining to any aspect of the field of micrographics

**AUDIENCE:** Members of National Micrographics Association

**PREFERRED TOPICS:** Technical articles on systems and case studies, computer output microfilm and scientific communications, standards information, educational opportunities, new product news.

**INAPPROPRIATE TOPICS:** Sales pitches for a particular product

**FEATURES:** New product news

**REVIEWS:** Yes
**STUDENT PAPERS:** No

**RESTRICTIONS:** None
**COVER LETTER:** Yes
**NUMBER OF COPIES:** 1
**STYLE:** Chicago
**FORMAT:** Standard
**ABSTRACT:** 150
**LENGTH:** 3,500
**INSTRUCTION FORM:** Yes

**ACKNOWLEDGED:** Yes
**REVIEW PROCESS:** Editorial board
**NOTIFICATION TIME:** 4-6 weeks

**CRITICISM:** No

**ACCEPTANCE RATE:** 80%
**REVISION:** Light
**EARLY PUBLICATION OPTION:** No
**COPYRIGHT POLICY:** Publisher
**FEE:** None
**REPRINTS:** 3-5 copies of issue
**PUBLICATION TIME LAG:** 2-4 months
**PROOFS:** No
**PAGE CHARGES:** No

JOURNAL TITLE: Journal of Research Communication Studies

SUBSCRIPTION ADDRESS: Elsevier Scientific Publishers, P.O. Box 211, 1000 AE Amsterdam, The Netherlands

PRICE: $43.90
CIRCULATION: Not given
AFFILIATION: None
INDEXED/ABSTRACTED: IH, LISA

FREQUENCY: Quarterly

MANUSCRIPT ADDRESS: Prof. A. J. Meadows, Primary Communications Research Centre, University of Leicester, Leicester LE1 7 RH, England

EDITORIAL POLICY: All aspects of the communication of research and development work

AUDIENCE: Researchers, publishers, librarians, information scientists

PREFERRED TOPICS: Articles which discuss the findings of researchers in terms comprehensible to non-specialists

INAPPROPRIATE TOPICS: Not given

FEATURES: Series of papers or short commentaries looking at the same topic from differing viewpoints

REVIEWS: Yes

STUDENT PAPERS: No

RESTRICTIONS: None
COVER LETTER: Not essential
NUMBER OF COPIES: 3
STYLE: House
FORMAT: Standard

ABSTRACT: 400
LENGTH: 5,000-7,000
INSTRUCTION FORM: Yes

ACKNOWLEDGED: Yes
REVIEW PROCESS: Editorial board and external reviewers

NOTIFICATION TIME: 2-3 months

CRITICISM: No

ACCEPTANCE RATE: 94%
REVISION: Medium
EARLY PUBLICATION OPTION: No
COPYRIGHT POLICY: Publisher
FEE: None
REPRINTS: 50

PUBLICATION TIME LAG: 2-6 months
PROOFS: No
PAGE CHARGES: No

**JOURNAL TITLE:** Journal of Systems Management

**SUBSCRIPTION ADDRESS:** Journal of Systems Management, 24587 Bagley Road, Cleveland, OH 44138

**PRICE:** $15
**CIRCULATION:** 14,000
**AFFILIATION:** Association for Systems Management
**INDEXED/ABSTRACTED:** LISA

**FREQUENCY:** Monthly

**MANUSCRIPT ADDRESS:** J. W. Haslett, 24587 Bagley Road, Cleveland, OH 44138

**EDITORIAL POLICY:** Dedicated to the advancement of information resources management

**AUDIENCE:** Business systems analysts

**PREFERRED TOPICS:** Business systems, information processing, forms design, management information systems

**INAPPROPRIATE TOPICS:** Not given

**FEATURES:** Not given

**REVIEWS:** Infrequent

**STUDENT PAPERS:** No

**RESTRICTIONS:** None
**COVER LETTER:** Yes
**NUMBER OF COPIES:** 3
**STYLE:** Not given
**FORMAT:** Standard

**ABSTRACT:** No
**LENGTH:** 1,200
**INSTRUCTION FORM:** Yes

**ACKNOWLEDGED:** Yes
**REVIEW PROCESS:** Editorial board

**NOTIFICATION TIME:** 1 month

**CRITICISM:** Yes

**ACCEPTANCE RATE:** 30%
**REVISION:** Light
**EARLY PUBLICATION OPTION:** No
**COPYRIGHT POLICY:** Publisher
**FEE:** $25
**REPRINTS:** Some issues of journal

**PUBLICATION TIME LAG:** 3 months
**PROOFS:** No

**PAGE CHARGES:** No

**JOURNAL TITLE:** Just b' TWX Us

**SUBSCRIPTION ADDRESS:** Interlibrary Loan, University Libraries, University of Colorado at Boulder, Boulder, CO 80309

**PRICE:** $5 for 2 years
**CIRCULATION:** 375
**AFFILIATION:** None
**INDEXED/ABSTRACTED:** Not given

**FREQUENCY:** Occasional

**MANUSCRIPT ADDRESS:** Virginia Boucher, Interlibrary Loan, University of Colorado at Boulder, Boulder, CO 80309

**EDITORIAL POLICY:** Practical interlibrary loan information

**AUDIENCE:** Interlibrary loan librarians

**PREFERRED TOPICS:** Material of interest to interlibrary loan librarians

**INAPPROPRIATE TOPICS:** None given

**FEATURES:** Choice items from the information explosion (bibliography)

**REVIEWS:** Very few
**STUDENT PAPERS:** No

**RESTRICTIONS:** None
**COVER LETTER:** Yes
**NUMBER OF COPIES:** 1
**STYLE:** House
**FORMAT:** Standard

**ABSTRACT:** No
**LENGTH:** 2-3 pages
**INSTRUCTION FORM:** Yes

**ACKNOWLEDGED:** Yes
**REVIEW PROCESS:** Editor

**NOTIFICATION TIME:** Varies

**CRITICISM:** No

**ACCEPTANCE RATE:** 95%
**REVISION:** Medium
**EARLY PUBLICATION OPTION:** No
**COPYRIGHT POLICY:** Not copyrighted
**FEE:** None
**REPRINTS:** None

**PUBLICATION TIME LAG:** Varies
**PROOFS:** No

**PAGE CHARGES:** No

JOURNAL TITLE: Law Library Journal

SUBSCRIPTION ADDRESS: American Association of Law Libraries, 53 West Jackson Blvd., Chicago, IL 60604

PRICE: $25
CIRCULATION: 3,640
AFFILIATION: American Association of Law Libraries
INDEXED/ABSTRACTED: ILP, LISA, LL, SSCI

FREQUENCY: Quarterly

MANUSCRIPT ADDRESS: Lorraine A. Kulpa, American Association of Law Libraries, 53 West Jackson Blvd., Chicago, IL 60604

EDITORIAL POLICY: A record of the work of the American Association of Law Libraries and the development of legal bibliography and law library science

AUDIENCE: Law and nonlaw librarians, members of the practicing bar and the judiciary in the U.S. and abroad

PREFERRED TOPICS: Those concerned with the law

INAPPROPRIATE TOPICS: N/A

FEATURES: Questions & Answers, Current Comments, Legal Humor, Annual Statistics

REVIEWS: No

STUDENT PAPERS: No

RESTRICTIONS: None
COVER LETTER: Yes
NUMBER OF COPIES: 2
STYLE: GPO
FORMAT: Standard

ABSTRACT: 50
LENGTH: Not given
INSTRUCTION FORM: Yes

ACKNOWLEDGED: Discretionary
REVIEW PROCESS: Editor

NOTIFICATION TIME: 1-3 months

CRITICISM: Seldom

ACCEPTANCE RATE: 99.9%
REVISION: Light
EARLY PUBLICATION OPTION: No
COPYRIGHT POLICY: Publisher
FEE: None
REPRINTS: 2 copies of issue; reprints may be purchased

PUBLICATION TIME LAG: 6-9 months
PROOFS: No

PAGE CHARGES: No

**JOURNAL TITLE:** Learning Today

**SUBSCRIPTION ADDRESS:** Learning Today, Box 956, Norman, OK 73070

**PRICE:** $14
**CIRCULATION:** 2,500
**AFFILIATION:** Library-College Associates, Inc.
**INDEXED/ABSTRACTED:** CARLD, CC, EdI, LISA, LL

**FREQUENCY:** Quarterly

**MANUSCRIPT ADDRESS:** Howard Clayton, Learning Today, School of Library Science, University of Oklahoma, Box 956, Norman, OK 73096

**EDITORIAL POLICY:** To increase awareness of, and appreciation for, the role of all study tools in the learning process

**AUDIENCE:** Educators at all levels of the system

**PREFERRED TOPICS:** Articles that deal with personalizing study through self-directed use of educational resources

**INAPPROPRIATE TOPICS:** Not given

**FEATURES:** Not given

**REVIEWS:** Yes

**STUDENT PAPERS:** Yes

**RESTRICTIONS:** None
**COVER LETTER:** No
**NUMBER OF COPIES:** 1
**STYLE:** House
**FORMAT:** Standard

**ABSTRACT:** No
**LENGTH:** 1,500-2,000
**INSTRUCTION FORM:** Not given

**ACKNOWLEDGED:** Yes
**REVIEW PROCESS:** Not given

**NOTIFICATION TIME:** 2 weeks

**CRITICISM:** No

**ACCEPTANCE RATE:** 25%
**REVISION:** Not given
**EARLY PUBLICATION OPTION:** No
**COPYRIGHT POLICY:** Publisher
**FEE:** None
**REPRINTS:** As many copies of issue as requested

**PUBLICATION TIME LAG:** Varies
**PROOFS:** Not given
**PAGE CHARGES:** No

**JOURNAL TITLE:** Legal Reference Services Quarterly
**SUBSCRIPTION ADDRESS:** Haworth Press, 28 East 22 Street, New York, NY 10010

**PRICE:** $25
**CIRCULATION:** Not given (new journal)
**AFFILIATION:** None
**INDEXED/ABSTRACTED:** Not

**FREQUENCY:** Quarterly

**MANUSCRIPT ADDRESS:** Robert C. Berring, University of Washington Law Library, 1100 NE Campus Parkway, JB-20, Seattle, WA 98105

**EDITORIAL POLICY:** Articles to aid the reference librarian who works with legal materials

**AUDIENCE:** Reference and public service librarians

**PREFERRED TOPICS:** Guides to research in subject specialty areas; bibliographies of current materials, new looks at research material and methodology

**INAPPROPRIATE TOPICS:** Not given

**FEATURES:** Not given

**REVIEWS:** Not given

**STUDENT PAPERS:** Yes

**RESTRICTIONS:** None
**COVER LETTER:** Yes
**NUMBER OF COPIES:** 1
**STYLE:** House
**FORMAT:** Standard

**ABSTRACT:** No
**LENGTH:** Not given
**INSTRUCTION FORM:** Yes

**ACKNOWLEDGED:** Yes
**REVIEW PROCESS:** Editorial board

**NOTIFICATION TIME:** Not given

**CRITICISM:** Sometimes

**ACCEPTANCE RATE:** N/A
**REVISION:** Medium
**EARLY PUBLICATION OPTION:** No
**COPYRIGHT POLICY:** Not given
**FEE:** None
**REPRINTS:** Not given

**PUBLICATION TIME LAG:** Not given
**PROOFS:** Yes
**PAGE CHARGES:** No

**JOURNAL TITLE:** Librarians for Social Change

**SUBSCRIPTION ADDRESS:** John L. Noyce, P.O. Box 450, Brighton, Sussex, BN1 8GR, England

**PRICE:** $8
**CIRCULATION:** 500
**AFFILIATION:** None
**INDEXED/ABSTRACTED:** BAPI, CALL, LISA

**FREQUENCY:** 3 x a year

**MANUSCRIPT ADDRESS:** John L. Noyce, P.O. Box 450, Brighton, Sussex, BN1 8GR, England

**EDITORIAL POLICY:** A magazine for and about librarians committed to social change, primarily in Britain

**AUDIENCE:** Librarians

**PREFERRED TOPICS:** See editorial policy statement

**INAPPROPRIATE TOPICS:** Poetry

**FEATURES:** Alternative libraries; libraries and new technology

**REVIEWS:** Yes

**STUDENT PAPERS:** N/A

**RESTRICTIONS:** Not given
**COVER LETTER:** Yes
**NUMBER OF COPIES:** 1
**STYLE:** House
**FORMAT:** Standard

**ABSTRACT:** Yes
**LENGTH:** 500-1,500
**INSTRUCTION FORM:** No

**ACKNOWLEDGED:** Yes
**REVIEW PROCESS:** Editor

**NOTIFICATION TIME:** Varies

**CRITICISM:** Sometimes

**ACCEPTANCE RATE:** 95%
**REVISION:** Light
**EARLY PUBLICATION OPTION:** No
**COPYRIGHT POLICY:** Publisher
**FEE:** None
**REPRINTS:** 1 copy of issue

**PUBLICATION TIME LAG:** 3-9 months
**PROOFS:** No
**PAGE CHARGES:** No

**JOURNAL TITLE:** Library and Archival Security

**SUBSCRIPTION ADDRESS:** Haworth Press, 28 East 22 Street, New York, NY 10010

**PRICE:** $28
**CIRCULATION:** 800
**AFFILIATION:** None
**INDEXED/ABSTRACTED:** CALL, FRAR, IPARL, LISA, LL

**FREQUENCY:** 3 X a year

**MANUSCRIPT ADDRESS:** Peter Gellatly, Library & Archival Security, 310 Third Street, New Westminster, BC, Canada V3L 2R9

**EDITORIAL POLICY:** Articles on all facets of preservation and conservation, and on security

**AUDIENCE:** Librarians, archivists, security agents

**PREFERRED TOPICS:** Electronic security devices, other security devices, fines, preservation of materials, conservation and security training, detection and prevention of library crimes

**INAPPROPRIATE TOPICS:** Unsolicited book reviews

**FEATURES:** "New Products"--a column in which new products are described and evaluated as to library and archival usefulness

**REVIEWS:** Only in own area      **STUDENT PAPERS:** No

**RESTRICTIONS:** None
**COVER LETTER:** Yes
**NUMBER OF COPIES:** 3
**STYLE:** Chicago
**FORMAT:** Standard

**ABSTRACT:** 100
**LENGTH:** 500-3,500
**INSTRUCTION FORM:** Yes

**ACKNOWLEDGED:** Yes
**REVIEW PROCESS:** Editorial board and external reviewers

**NOTIFICATION TIME:** 2-8 weeks

**CRITICISM:** Rarely

**ACCEPTANCE RATE:** 50%
**REVISION:** Light
**EARLY PUBLICATION OPTION:** No
**COPYRIGHT POLICY:** Publisher
**FEE:** None
**REPRINTS:** 10

**PUBLICATION TIME LAG:** 6-12 months
**PROOFS:** Yes

**PAGE CHARGES:** No

**JOURNAL TITLE:** Library History

**SUBSCRIPTION ADDRESS:** Mis V.A.A. Fletcher, c/o Law Library, King's College, Strand, London WC2R 2LS, England

**PRICE:** $12
**FREQUENCY:** Semiannual
**CIRCULATION:** 1,600
**AFFILIATION:** Library Association, Library History Group
**INDEXED/ABSTRACTED:** BHI, HA, LISA, LL

**MANUSCRIPT ADDRESS:** P. S. Morrish, c/o Brotherton Library, University of Leeds, LS2 9JT England

**EDITORIAL POLICY:** Scholarly articles on the history of British and European libraries. Articles are based on research using unpublished source material

**AUDIENCE:** Librarians, book collectors, historians

**PREFERRED TOPICS:** History of British and European libraries

**INAPPROPRIATE TOPICS:** No comment

**FEATURES:** Surveys of ancient literature, archives relating to library history

**REVIEWS:** Yes
**STUDENT PAPERS:** No

**RESTRICTIONS:** None
**COVER LETTER:** Yes
**NUMBER OF COPIES:** 2
**STYLE:** Not specified
**FORMAT:** Standard
**ABSTRACT:** No
**LENGTH:** Variable
**INSTRUCTION FORM:** No

**ACKNOWLEDGED:** Yes
**REVIEW PROCESS:** Editor
**NOTIFICATION TIME:** Varies

**CRITICISM:** Depends on circumstances

**ACCEPTANCE RATE:** No data
**PUBLICATION TIME LAG:** 2 years
**REVISION:** Depends on circumstances
**PROOFS:** Sometimes
**EARLY PUBLICATION OPTION:** No
**PAGE CHARGES:** No
**COPYRIGHT POLICY:** Author and publisher
**FEE:** None
**REPRINTS:** None

114 / ALPHABETICAL LISTING OF JOURNALS

JOURNAL TITLE: Library History Review
SUBSCRIPTION ADDRESS: K. K. Roy (Private) Ltd., 55 Gariahat Road, P. O. Box 10210, Calcutta 700 019 India

PRICE: $25
CIRCULATION: 1,350
AFFILIATION: International Agency for Research in Library History
INDEXED/ABSTRACTED: Not
FREQUENCY: Quarterly

MANUSCRIPT ADDRESS: Dr. Kuldip Kumar Roy, (Private) Ltd., 55 Gariahat Road, Box 10210, Calcutta 700 019, India

EDITORIAL POLICY: Aims to integrate the research of library historians on an international plane

AUDIENCE: Professionals involved in international library development
PREFERRED TOPICS: Articles on the history and bibliography of libraries and related subjects

INAPPROPRIATE TOPICS: Current developments in libraries

FEATURES: History of libraries and biographical articles on eminent librarians from ancient times until now

REVIEWS: Yes
STUDENT PAPERS: Yes

RESTRICTIONS: None
COVER LETTER: Yes
NUMBER OF COPIES: 2
STYLE: Chicago
FORMAT: Standard
ABSTRACT: 100
LENGTH: 10,000
INSTRUCTION FORM: Yes

ACKNOWLEDGED: Yes (SASE)
REVIEW PROCESS: Editorial board and external reviewers
CRITICISM: No
NOTIFICATION TIME: 2 months

ACCEPTANCE RATE: 60%
REVISION: Medium
EARLY PUBLICATION OPTION: Yes
COPYRIGHT POLICY: Author
FEE: None
REPRINTS: 25
PUBLICATION TIME LAG: 9-12 months
PROOFS: Yes
PAGE CHARGES: No

**JOURNAL TITLE:** Library Journal

**SUBSCRIPTION ADDRESS:** R. R. Bowker Co., Subscription Department, P.O. Box 67, Whitinsville, MA 01588

**PRICE:** $27
**CIRCULATION:** 30,000
**AFFILIATION:** None
**INDEXED/ABSTRACTED:** BRD, BRI, CBRC, EdI, LISA, LL, MI

**FREQUENCY:** Semimonthly

**MANUSCRIPT ADDRESS:** John Berry, Library Journal, 1180 Avenue of the Americas, New York, NY 10036

**EDITORIAL POLICY:** A multi-purpose journal which contains articles on all aspects of librarianship and extensive reviews

**AUDIENCE:** Professional librarians, library workers, trustees

**PREFERRED TOPICS:** Particularly those articles that relate library service to the larger social issues

**INAPPROPRIATE TOPICS:** Library poetry, unsolicited book reviews

**FEATURES:** Not given

**REVIEWS:** Yes

**STUDENT PAPERS:** Yes

**RESTRICTIONS:** None
**COVER LETTER:** Yes
**NUMBER OF COPIES:** 2
**STYLE:** Turabian
**FORMAT:** Standard

**ABSTRACT:** No
**LENGTH:** 2-2,500
**INSTRUCTION FORM:** Yes

**ACKNOWLEDGED:** Yes
**REVIEW PROCESS:** Staff editors

**NOTIFICATION TIME:** 1-4 months

**CRITICISM:** Sometimes

**ACCEPTANCE RATE:** 10%
**REVISION:** Varies
**EARLY PUBLICATION OPTION:** No
**COPYRIGHT POLICY:** Author; publisher may contract for serial rights
**FEE:** $50-$350
**REPRINTS:** 6 copies of issue

**PUBLICATION TIME LAG:** 1-12 months
**PROOFS:** No
**PAGE CHARGES:** No

**JOURNAL TITLE:** Library Management News

**SUBSCRIPTION ADDRESS:** Center for Library and Information Management, Department of Library and Information Studies, Loughborough University, Loughborough, Leicestershire LE11 3TU, England

**PRICE:** Free **FREQUENCY:** Quarterly
**CIRCULATION:** 600
**AFFILIATION:** British Library Research and Development Department
**INDEXED/ABSTRACTED:** Not given

**MANUSCRIPT ADDRESS:** Linda Stuart, Library Management News, Department of Library and Information Studies, Loughborough University, Loughborough, Leicestershire LE11 3TU, England
**EDITORIAL POLICY:** Intended primarily as a vehicle for communication, debate and discussion between library managers

**AUDIENCE:** Library managers

**PREFERRED TOPICS:** Anything on library management

**INAPPROPRIATE TOPICS:** Not given

**FEATURES:** Not given

**REVIEWS:** Yes **STUDENT PAPERS:** No

**RESTRICTIONS:** None
**COVER LETTER:** No **ABSTRACT:** No
**NUMBER OF COPIES:** 1 **LENGTH:** 1,500-2,000
**STYLE:** No requirements **INSTRUCTION FORM:** No
**FORMAT:** No requirements

**ACKNOWLEDGED:** Yes **NOTIFICATION TIME:** 1 day
**REVIEW PROCESS:** Editor

**CRITICISM:** No

**ACCEPTANCE RATE:** 90% **PUBLICATION TIME LAG:** 2-8 weeks
**REVISION:** Light **PROOFS:** No
**EARLY PUBLICATION OPTION:** No **PAGE CHARGES:** No
**COPYRIGHT POLICY:** Publisher
**FEE:** None
**REPRINTS:** 2

ALPHABETICAL LISTING OF JOURNALS / 117

JOURNAL TITLE: Library PR News

SUBSCRIPTION ADDRESS: Library PR News, P.O. Box 687, Bloomfield, NJ 07003

PRICE: $15
CIRCULATION: 3,000
AFFILIATION: None
INDEXED/ABSTRACTED: Not given

FREQUENCY: Bimonthly

MANUSCRIPT ADDRESS: Phillip J. Bradbury, Library PR News, P.O. Box 687, Bloomfield, NJ 07003

EDITORIAL POLICY: A newsletter providing practical, nuts-and-bolts information on all aspects of library PR, exhibits and displays

AUDIENCE: Public relations specialists, display artists

PREFERRED TOPICS: Articles on publicity, public relations, exhibits and displays as they relate to libraries

INAPPROPRIATE TOPICS: Scholarly essays on the nature of advertising, motivational research, etc.

FEATURES: PR idea exchange; Exhibit Pick (photo and explication of library displays)

REVIEWS: Yes

STUDENT PAPERS: No

RESTRICTIONS: None
COVER LETTER: Yes
NUMBER OF COPIES: 1
STYLE: MLA
FORMAT: Standard

ABSTRACT: No
LENGTH: 1,000-1,500
INSTRUCTION FORM: Yes

ACKNOWLEDGED: Yes (SASE)
REVIEW PROCESS: Editorial board

NOTIFICATION TIME: 2-3 weeks

CRITICISM: No

ACCEPTANCE RATE: Not given
REVISION: Medium
EARLY PUBLICATION OPTION: No
COPYRIGHT POLICY: Publisher
FEE: Occasionally, made on publication
REPRINTS: 2 copies of issue

PUBLICATION TIME LAG: 4-8 months
PROOFS: No

PAGE CHARGES: No

JOURNAL TITLE: Library Quarterly

SUBSCRIPTION ADDRESS: University of Chicago Press, 11030 S. Langley Ave., Chicago, IL 60628

PRICE: $15
CIRCULATION: 3,700
AFFILIATION: Graduate Library School, University of Chicago
INDEXED/ABSTRACTED: AHL, BRD, BRI, CIJE, HA, ISA, LISA, LL

FREQUENCY: Quarterly

MANUSCRIPT ADDRESS: W. Boyd Rayward, Library Quarterly, Graduate Library School, University of Chicago, 1100 57th St., Chicago, IL 60637

EDITORIAL POLICY: A journal of investigation and discussion in the field of library science

AUDIENCE: Librarians, library administrators, library educators, and library students
PREFERRED TOPICS: Research articles, theoretical articles, review articles

INAPPROPRIATE TOPICS: Not given

FEATURES: Annual conference issue (papers presented, by invitation, at the annual conference of the Graduate Library School). Solicited book reviews in each issue
REVIEWS: Yes
STUDENT PAPERS: No

RESTRICTIONS: None
COVER LETTER: Yes
NUMBER OF COPIES: 2
STYLE: Chicago
FORMAT: Standard

ABSTRACT: 100-150
LENGTH: Not given
INSTRUCTION FORM: Yes, style requirements in back of each issue

ACKNOWLEDGED: Yes
REVIEW PROCESS: Editorial board

NOTIFICATION TIME: 6 weeks

CRITICISM: In some cases

ACCEPTANCE RATE: 15-20
REVISION: Light
EARLY PUBLICATION OPTION: No
COPYRIGHT POLICY: Publisher
FEE: None
REPRINTS: 50

PUBLICATION TIME LAG: 6 months
PROOFS: No
PAGE CHARGES: No

**JOURNAL TITLE:** Library Research

**SUBSCRIPTION ADDRESS:** Ablex Publishing Corporation, 355 Chestnut St., Norwood, NJ 07648

**PRICE:** $19.50
**CIRCULATION:** Not given
**AFFILIATION:** None
**INDEXED/ABSTRACTED:** Not given

**FREQUENCY:** Quarterly

**MANUSCRIPT ADDRESS:** Editor, Library Research, Central University Library C-075, University of California, San Diego, La Jolla, CA 92093

**EDITORIAL POLICY:** A scholarly journal which provides access to carefully referred reports of completed research and reviews of research-oriented topics in all areas of librarianship

**AUDIENCE:** Librarians and information scientists in all fields of library and information science

**PREFERRED TOPICS:** Results of library and library-related research; reports of both mission-oriented research and basic research; reviews of important research oriented topics

**INAPPROPRIATE TOPICS:** Articles based on opinion rather than research

**FEATURES:** Review articles on research related subjects of particular current interest

**REVIEWS:** Yes

**STUDENT PAPERS:** Yes

**RESTRICTIONS:** None
**COVER LETTER:** Yes
**NUMBER OF COPIES:** 3
**STYLE:** House
**FORMAT:** Standard

**ABSTRACT:** 100-150
**LENGTH:** 3,000-8,000
**INSTRUCTION FORM:** Yes

**ACKNOWLEDGED:** Yes
**REVIEW PROCESS:** Editorial board and external reviewers

**NOTIFICATION TIME:** 1-2 months

**CRITICISM:** Yes

**ACCEPTANCE RATE:** 40%
**REVISION:** Light
**EARLY PUBLICATION OPTION:** No
**COPYRIGHT POLICY:** Publisher
**FEE:** $50 for research articles; $150 for review articles
**REPRINTS:** None

**PUBLICATION TIME LAG:** 3-6 months
**PROOFS:** Yes
**PAGE CHARGES:** No

**JOURNAL TITLE:** Library Resources & Technical Services

**SUBSCRIPTION ADDRESS:** American Library Association, 50 E. Huron St., Chicago, IL 60611

**PRICE:** $7.50
**CIRCULATION:** 12,000
**AFFILIATION:** ALA Resources and Technical Services Division
**INDEXED/ABSTRACTED:** BRD, BRI, CALL, CIJE, HLI, LISA, LL, SCI
**FREQUENCY:** Quarterly

**MANUSCRIPT ADDRESS:** Elizabeth Tate, 1145 Framland Drive, Rockville, MD 20852

**EDITORIAL POLICY:** Contains articles on technical services, library acquisitions, cataloging, calssification, serials and preservation of library materials

**AUDIENCE:** Librarians

**PREFERRED TOPICS:** Well written, readable articles that further the solution of problems confronting technical services librarians

**INAPPROPRIATE TOPICS:** Articles that air a pet peeve without offering constructive suggestions for improvement; institution specific articles that are historical accounts

**FEATURES:** Summer issue is devoted to articles reviewing the major events and publications of the previous calendar year in several areas of concern.

**REVIEWS:** Yes
**STUDENT PAPERS:** No

**RESTRICTIONS:** None
**COVER LETTER:** Yes
**NUMBER OF COPIES:** 3
**STYLE:** Chicago
**FORMAT:** Standard
**ABSTRACT:** 100-150
**LENGTH:** 15-20 pages
**INSTRUCTION FORM:** Yes

**ACKNOWLEDGED:** Yes
**REVIEW PROCESS:** Editorial board and external reviewers
**NOTIFICATION TIME:** Varies

**CRITICISM:** No

**ACCEPTANCE RATE:** 50-60%
**REVISION:** Varies
**EARLY PUBLICATION OPTION:** No
**COPYRIGHT POLICY:** Publisher
**FEE:** None
**REPRINTS:** 2 copies of issue
**PUBLICATION TIME LAG:** 4-12 months
**PROOFS:** Yes
**PAGE CHARGES:** No

**JOURNAL TITLE:** The Library Scene

**SUBSCRIPTION ADDRESS:** The Library Scene, 322 Stuart St., Boston, MA 02116

**PRICE:** $8
**CIRCULATION:** 13,000
**AFFILIATION:** Library Binding Institute
**INDEXED/ABSTRACTED:** LL

**FREQUENCY:** Quarterly

**MANUSCRIPT ADDRESS:** Beverly Adamonis, The Library Scene, Library Binding Institute, 50 Congress St., Suite 633, Boston, MA 02109

**EDITORIAL POLICY:** Articles which center around the theme of binding, preservation and conservation of library materials, restoration of library materials or related topics

**AUDIENCE:** Librarians, library science students, binders, preservationists, conservationists

**PREFERRED TOPICS:** Those which center on binding, prolonging the useful life of library materials, restoration, preservation, conservation, etc.

**INAPPROPRIATE TOPICS:** Not given

**FEATURES:** Profiles of library science schools, private, special and public libraries; profiles of binders, preservationists, conservationists

**REVIEWS:** Yes
**STUDENT PAPERS:** Yes

**RESTRICTIONS:** None
**COVER LETTER:** Yes
**NUMBER OF COPIES:** 1
**STYLE:** Not specified
**FORMAT:** Standard

**ABSTRACT:** No
**LENGTH:** 4-6 pages
**INSTRUCTION FORM:**

**ACKNOWLEDGED:** Yes
**REVIEW PROCESS:** Editor

**NOTIFICATION TIME:** 2 months

**CRITICISM:** No

**ACCEPTANCE RATE:** 75%
**REVISION:** Varies
**EARLY PUBLICATION OPTION:** No
**COPYRIGHT POLICY:** Publisher
**FEE:** None
**REPRINTS:** 1 copy of issue

**PUBLICATION TIME LAG:** 1-5 months
**PROOFS:** No

**PAGE CHARGES:** No

**JOURNAL TITLE:** Library Trends

**SUBSCRIPTION ADDRESS:** Library Trends, University of Illinois Press, Journals Department, 54 E. Gregory, P.O. Box 5081, Station A, Champaign, IL 61820

**PRICE:** $16
**FREQUENCY:** Quarterly
**CIRCULATION:** 5,000
**AFFILIATION:** University of Illinois, Grad. School of Lib. Sci.
**INDEXED/ABSTRACTED:** CC, CIJE, LISA, LL, PAIS, SSCI

**MANUSCRIPT ADDRESS:** Charles Davis, Publications Office, Library Trends, 215 Armory Building, University of Illinois Graduate School of Library Science, Champaign, IL 61820

**EDITORIAL POLICY:** Each issue is concerned with a single aspect of library science. An editor is selected for each issue, depending on his/her knowledge of the topic.

**AUDIENCE:** Scholarly librarians, students, faculty, information scientists

**PREFERRED TOPICS:** Articles concerned with significant conditions and movements in the field, which evidence intensive coverage of both literature and practice

**INAPPROPRIATE TOPICS:** Unsolicited works

**FEATURES:** None

**REVIEWS:** No
**STUDENT PAPERS:** No

**RESTRICTIONS:** Invited authors
**COVER LETTER:** Yes
**NUMBER OF COPIES:** 1
**STYLE:** Chicago
**FORMAT:** Standard
**ABSTRACT:** Yes
**LENGTH:** 20 pages
**INSTRUCTION FORM:** Yes

**ACKNOWLEDGED:** Yes
**REVIEW PROCESS:** Editorial board
**NOTIFICATION TIME:** N/A

**CRITICISM:** No

**ACCEPTANCE RATE:** 100%
**REVISION:** Medium
**EARLY PUBLICATION OPTION:** No
**COPYRIGHT POLICY:** Publisher
**FEE:** None
**REPRINTS:** 50
**PUBLICATION TIME LAG:** 21 months
**PROOFS:** Yes
**PAGE CHARGES:** No

**JOURNAL TITLE:** The Lion and the Unicorn

**SUBSCRIPTION ADDRESS:** The Lion and the Unicorn, Department of English, Brooklyn College, Brooklyn, NY 11210

**PRICE:** $6
**CIRCULATION:** 900
**AFFILIATION:** None
**INDEXED/ABSTRACTED:** AHCI, MLA

**FREQUENCY:** Semiannual

**MANUSCRIPT ADDRESS:** Geraldine DeLuca & Roni Natov, Department of English, Brooklyn College, Brooklyn, NY 11210

**EDITORIAL POLICY:** A journal of critical articles on children's literature. Each issue is theme centered and themes are announced in advance.

**AUDIENCE:** Teachers of children's literature, librarians, elementary and secondary teachers, students

**PREFERRED TOPICS:** Articles that are critical and informative rather than purely scholarly in nature.

**INAPPROPRIATE TOPICS:** Articles of purely historical interest, i.e., articles about books, poems, etc. that children no longer read

**FEATURES:** Each issue is devoted to a particular theme; interviews with authors

**REVIEWS:** Yes

**STUDENT PAPERS:** No

**RESTRICTIONS:** None
**COVER LETTER:** Yes
**NUMBER OF COPIES:** 1
**STYLE:** MLA
**FORMAT:** Standard

**ABSTRACT:** No
**LENGTH:** 10-30 pages
**INSTRUCTION FORM:** Yes

**ACKNOWLEDGED:** Yes
**REVIEW PROCESS:** Editorial board

**NOTIFICATION TIME:** 2-6 months

**CRITICISM:** Yes

**ACCEPTANCE RATE:** 25%
**REVISION:** Medium
**EARLY PUBLICATION OPTION:** No
**COPYRIGHT POLICY:** Publisher
**FEE:** None
**REPRINTS:** 2 copies of issue

**PUBLICATION TIME LAG:** 6 months
**PROOFS:** No

**PAGE CHARGES:** No

JOURNAL TITLE: MELA Notes

SUBSCRIPTION ADDRESS: MELA Secretariat, Room 032 Main Library, The Ohio State University, 1858 Neil Avenue Mall, Columbus, OH 43210, Attn. Marsha McClintock

PRICE: $5
CIRCULATION: 300
AFFILIATION: Middle East Librarians Association
INDEXED/ABSTRACTED: Not given

FREQUENCY: 3 x a year

MANUSCRIPT ADDRESS: E. Christian Filstrup, Chief Oriental Division, New York Public Library, 5th Avenue and 42nd Street, New York, NY 10018

EDITORIAL POLICY: Articles of interest to Middle East scholars and librarians

AUDIENCE: Members of the Middle East Librarians Association

PREFERRED TOPICS: Works of library orientation, works on manuscripts, books in progress, current research

INAPPROPRIATE TOPICS: Not given

FEATURES: Not given

REVIEWS: Not given

STUDENT PAPERS: Not given

RESTRICTIONS: None
COVER LETTER: Yes
NUMBER OF COPIES: 1
STYLE: No recommendation
FORMAT: Standard

ABSTRACT: No
LENGTH: Not given
INSTRUCTION FORM: No

ACKNOWLEDGED: Yes
REVIEW PROCESS: Editorial board

NOTIFICATION TIME: 1 Month

CRITICISM: No

ACCEPTANCE RATE: 95%
REVISION: Light
EARLY PUBLICATION OPTION: Not given
COPYRIGHT POLICY: Not copyrighted
FEE: None
REPRINTS: None

PUBLICATION TIME LAG: up to 3 months
PROOFS: No
PAGE CHARGES: No

**JOURNAL TITLE:** MPLA Newsletter

**SUBSCRIPTION ADDRESS:** Joseph R. Edelen, I.D. Weeks Library, University of South Dakota, Vermillion, SD 57069

**PRICE:** $11
**CIRCULATION:** 600
**AFFILIATION:** Mountain Plains Library Association
**INDEXED/ABSTRACTED:** LL

**FREQUENCY:** Semimonthly

**MANUSCRIPT ADDRESS:** Blaine H. Hall, Mountain Plains Library Association, I.D. Weeks Library, University of South Dakota, Vermillion, SD 57069

**EDITORIAL POLICY:** The newsletter publishes short articles and news items of interest to and about the Mountain Plains region and the profession at large.

**AUDIENCE:** Librarians/media specialists in Mountain Plains region

**PREFERRED TOPICS:** Articles on innovations and library-related activities in MPLA region or the profession in general

**INAPPROPRIATE TOPICS:** Not given

**FEATURES:** News of library happenings in member states; continuing education opportunities; newly published materials; news of members' achievements

**REVIEWS:** No      **STUDENT PAPERS:** No

**RESTRICTIONS:** None
**COVER LETTER:** Yes
**NUMBER OF COPIES:** 1
**STYLE:** MLA
**FORMAT:** Standard

**ABSTRACT:** No
**LENGTH:** 6-8 pages
**INSTRUCTION FORM:** Yes

**ACKNOWLEDGED:** Yes
**REVIEW PROCESS:** Editor

**NOTIFICATION TIME:** 2 months

**CRITICISM:** Brief

**ACCEPTANCE RATE:** Unknown
**REVISION:** Medium
**EARLY PUBLICATION OPTION:** Yes
**COPYRIGHT POLICY:** Author
**FEE:** None
**REPRINTS:** 2 copies of issue

**PUBLICATION TIME LAG:** 2-4 months
**PROOFS:** If requested
**PAGE CHARGES:** No

**JOURNAL TITLE:** Media

**SUBSCRIPTION ADDRESS:** Materials Services Department, 127 Ninth Avenue N., Nashville, TN 37234

**PRICE:** $5.25
**FREQUENCY:** Quarterly
**CIRCULATION:** 17,000
**AFFILIATION:** Sunday School Board, Southern Baptist Convention
**INDEXED/ABSTRACTED:** SBPI

**MANUSCRIPT ADDRESS:** Wanda C. Lineberry, Media, 127 Ninth Avenue North, Nashville, TN 37234

**EDITORIAL POLICY:** To assist churches in the establishment and development of a media center

**AUDIENCE:** Church media center staff members

**PREFERRED TOPICS:** Articles relating to church media center development, administration, and promotion

**INAPPROPRIATE TOPICS:** Not given

**FEATURES:** Innovative media center promotional approaches; media clubs, media education

**REVIEWS:** Yes
**STUDENT PAPERS:** No

**RESTRICTIONS:** None
**COVER LETTER:** Yes
**NUMBER OF COPIES:** 1
**STYLE:** House
**FORMAT:** Not given
**ABSTRACT:** No
**LENGTH:** 600-1,200
**INSTRUCTION FORM:** Yes

**ACKNOWLEDGED:** Yes
**REVIEW PROCESS:** External reviewers
**NOTIFICATION TIME:** 3-4 weeks

**CRITICISM:** To some extent

**ACCEPTANCE RATE:** 90%
**REVISION:** Medium
**EARLY PUBLICATION OPTION:** No
**COPYRIGHT POLICY:** Publisher
**FEE:** $.035 per word
**REPRINTS:** 3 copies of issue
**PUBLICATION TIME LAG:** 10-12 months
**PROOFS:** No
**PAGE CHARGES:** No

JOURNAL TITLE: Media & Methods

SUBSCRIPTION ADDRESS: Media & Methods, North American Publishing Company, 401 N. Broad St., Philadelphia, PA 19108

PRICE: $11
CIRCULATION: 50,000
AFFILIATION: None
INDEXED/ABSTRACTED: Not given

FREQUENCY: 9 x a year

MANUSCRIPT ADDRESS: Anthony Prete, Media & Methods, North American Building, 401 North Broad Street, Philadelphia, PA 19109

EDITORIAL POLICY: Essay-type articles which emphasize a humanistic approach to the teaching/learning process; stresses student involvement in an atmosphere structured to spontaneity and self-directed discovery.

AUDIENCE: Classroom teachers and media center directors (librarians)

PREFERRED TOPICS: Innovative concepts, thematic approaches to a particular study area, and reflective type articles dealing with educational issues.

INAPPROPRIATE TOPICS: Materials written for other purposes (course outlines, research reports, term papers, etc.)

FEATURES: "Have You Discovered" descriptions of interesting, useful, and perhaps off-beat materials; "Soundings," highly personal statements on controversial topics

REVIEWS: Not given

STUDENT PAPERS: Yes

RESTRICTIONS: None
COVER LETTER: Yes
NUMBER OF COPIES: 1
STYLE: No recommendation
FORMAT: Standard

ABSTRACT: No
LENGTH: 1,000-2,500
INSTRUCTION FORM: Yes

ACKNOWLEDGED: Yes
REVIEW PROCESS: Editor

NOTIFICATION TIME: 6-8 weeks

CRITICISM: Yes

ACCEPTANCE RATE: Not given
REVISION: Medium
EARLY PUBLICATION OPTION: Not given
COPYRIGHT POLICY: Publisher
FEE: $35-$75
REPRINTS: Copies of issue

PUBLICATION TIME LAG: Not given
PROOFS:
PAGE CHARGES: Not given

**JOURNAL TITLE:** Medical Library Association Bulletin

**SUBSCRIPTION ADDRESS:** Medical Library Association, 919 N. Michigan Avenue, #3208, Chicago, IL 60611

**PRICE:** $45
**CIRCULATION:** 6,500
**AFFILIATION:** Medical Library Association
**INDEXED/ABSTRACTED:** BHM, CINL, CWHM, DA, HLI, IM, LISA, LL
**FREQUENCY:** Quarterly

**MANUSCRIPT ADDRESS:** Robert Lewis, Medical Library Association Bulletin, Biomedical Library, University of California, San Diego, La Jolla, CA 92093

**EDITORIAL POLICY:** Contributions of value to medical bibliography, medical librarianship, and the history of medical books, libraries, and librarians

**AUDIENCE:** Health sciences librarians

**PREFERRED TOPICS:** Administration, organization, and services of health sciences libraries

**INAPPROPRIATE TOPICS:** Annotated bibliographies

**FEATURES:** Not given

**REVIEWS:** Yes
**STUDENT PAPERS:** No

**RESTRICTIONS:** None
**COVER LETTER:** No
**NUMBER OF COPIES:** 3
**STYLE:** Chicago
**FORMAT:** Standard
**ABSTRACT LENGTH:** 150
**INSTRUCTION FORM:** Yes
25 pages

**ACKNOWLEDGED:** Yes
**REVIEW PROCESS:** Editorial board
**NOTIFICATION TIME:** 6 weeks

**CRITICISM:** Yes

**ACCEPTANCE RATE:** 60%
**REVISION:** Light
**EARLY PUBLICATION OPTION:** No
**COPYRIGHT POLICY:** Publisher
**FEE:** None
**REPRINTS:** None
**PUBLICATION TIME LAG:** 6 months
**PROOFS:** Yes
**PAGE CHARGES:** No

**JOURNAL TITLE:** Methods of Information in Medicine

**SUBSCRIPTION ADDRESS:** F. K. Schattauer Verlag GmbH, Lenzhalde 3 7000, Stuttgart 1, Federal Republic of Germany

**PRICE:** DM 114,40
**CIRCULATION:** 2,000
**AFFILIATION:** None
**INDEXED/ABSTRACTED:** CC

**FREQUENCY:** Quarterly

**MANUSCRIPT ADDRESS:** F. K. Schattauer Verlag GmbH, Lenzhalde 3 Postfach 2945, 7000 Stuttgart 1, W. Germany

**EDITORIAL POLICY:** Special journal of methodology in medical research, documentation, informatics and statistics

**AUDIENCE:** Institutes, medical doctors, hospitals, medical scientists

**PREFERRED TOPICS:** Research articles, theoretical articles, review articles, congress reports, bibliographies in the field of medical research

**INAPPROPRIATE TOPICS:** Not given

**FEATURES:** Progress in data processing in medicine

**REVIEWS:** Yes

**STUDENT PAPERS:** No

**RESTRICTIONS:** None
**COVER LETTER:** Yes
**NUMBER OF COPIES:** 2
**STYLE:** No recommendation
**FORMAT:** No recommendation

**ABSTRACT:** 1/2 page
**LENGTH:** 3-4,000
**INSTRUCTION FORM:** Yes

**ACKNOWLEDGED:** Yes
**REVIEW PROCESS:** Editorial board

**NOTIFICATION TIME:** 4-6 weeks

**CRITICISM:** Yes

**ACCEPTANCE RATE:** 50%
**REVISION:** Medium
**EARLY PUBLICATION OPTION:** No
**COPYRIGHT POLICY:** Publisher
**FEE:** None
**REPRINTS:** 50

**PUBLICATION TIME LAG:** 6-8 weeks
**PROOFS:** Yes

**PAGE CHARGES:** No

**JOURNAL TITLE:** Microform Review

**SUBSCRIPTION ADDRESS:** Microform Review, 520 Riverside Avenue, P.O. Box 405, Saugatuck Station, Westport, CT 06880

**PRICE:** $30
**CIRCULATION:** 1,300
**AFFILIATION:** None
**INDEXED/ABSTRACTED:** ISA, LISA, LL

**FREQUENCY:** Quarterly

**MANUSCRIPT ADDRESS:** Allen B. Veaner, Microform Review, 520 Riverside Avenue, P.O. Box 405, Saugatuck Station, Westport, CT 06880

**EDITORIAL POLICY:** To publish reviews of micropublications; to publish surveys and articles on the history, management, and utilization of microtext materials in libraries

**AUDIENCE:** Librarians, book selection officers, micropublishers

**PREFERRED TOPICS:** Management and use of microtext, scholarly historic surveys, reviews of microtext

**INAPPROPRIATE TOPICS:** Articles promoting a specific commercial product or system

**FEATURES:** "News & Comment," done by the editorial staff

**REVIEWS:** Yes

**STUDENT PAPERS:** No

**RESTRICTIONS:** None
**COVER LETTER:** Yes
**NUMBER OF COPIES:** 1
**STYLE:** No requirements
**FORMAT:** Standard

**ABSTRACT:** No
**LENGTH:** 2,000-5,000
**INSTRUCTION FORM:** Yes

**ACKNOWLEDGED:** Usually
**REVIEW PROCESS:** Editor

**NOTIFICATION TIME:** 1-4 months

**CRITICISM:** Sometimes

**ACCEPTANCE RATE:** Varies
**REVISION:** Varies
**EARLY PUBLICATION OPTION:** No
**COPYRIGHT POLICY:** Publisher
**FEE:** None
**REPRINTS:** 2 copies of issue; 10 copies of article

**PUBLICATION TIME LAG:** 4-6 months
**PROOFS:** Yes
**PAGE CHARGES:** No

JOURNAL TITLE: Midwestern Archivist

SUBSCRIPTION ADDRESS: James E. Fogerty, MAC Secretary-Treasurer, Minnesota Historical Society, 1500 Mississippi Street, St. Paul, MN 55101

PRICE: $7
CIRCULATION: 600
AFFILIATION: Midwest Archives Conference
INDEXED/ABSTRACTED: AHL, HA

FREQUENCY: Semiannual

MANUSCRIPT ADDRESS: Mary Lynn Ritzenthaler, University of Illinois, Chicago Circle, Box 8198, Chicago, IL 60680

EDITORIAL POLICY: Concerned with issues and problems confronting the contemporary archivist

AUDIENCE: Practicing archivists and others interested in archival materials, practices, and issues
PREFERRED TOPICS: Articles, essays, and reports on archival theory and current practice

INAPPROPRIATE TOPICS: Student essays and term papers for archival management courses, and reports of limited applicability

FEATURES: Not given

REVIEWS: Yes

STUDENT PAPERS: No

RESTRICTIONS: None
COVER LETTER: Yes
NUMBER OF COPIES: 1
STYLE: Chicago
FORMAT: Standard

ABSTRACT: No
LENGTH: 3,4,500
INSTRUCTION FORM: Not given

ACKNOWLEDGED: Yes
REVIEW PROCESS: Editorial board

NOTIFICATION TIME: 8 weeks

CRITICISM: Yes

ACCEPTANCE RATE: 40-50%
REVISION: Medium
EARLY PUBLICATION OPTION: No
COPYRIGHT POLICY: Author at present, policy not fully developed
FEE: None
REPRINTS: 2 copies of issue

PUBLICATION TIME LAG: 3-12 months
PROOFS: No

PAGE CHARGES: No

JOURNAL TITLE: NLA Newsletter

SUBSCRIPTION ADDRESS: NLA Newsletter, P.O. Box 586, Alma, MI 48801

PRICE: $12
CIRCULATION: 1,200
AFFILIATION: National Librarians Association
INDEXED/ABSTRACTED: Not

FREQUENCY: Quarterly

MANUSCRIPT ADDRESS: Peter Dollard, The National Librarian, The Library, Alma College, Alma, MI 48801

EDITORIAL POLICY: Articles and news reports of concern to professional librarians

AUDIENCE: NLA members and other librarians

PREFERRED TOPICS: Articles related to the definition, promotion, and protection of the professional concerns of librarians

INAPPROPRIATE TOPICS: The technical aspects of librarianship

FEATURES: Serial bibliography on professionalism

REVIEWS: Yes                     STUDENT PAPERS: No

RESTRICTIONS: None
COVER LETTER: Yes
NUMBER OF COPIES: 1
STYLE: No recommendation
FORMAT: No requirements

ABSTRACT: No
LENGTH: 2,500
INSTRUCTION FORM: Yes

ACKNOWLEDGED: Yes
REVIEW PROCESS: Not given

NOTIFICATION TIME: 1 month

CRITICISM: Yes

ACCEPTANCE RATE: Not given
REVISION: Medium
EARLY PUBLICATION OPTION: No
COPYRIGHT POLICY: Publisher
FEE: None
REPRINTS: 5 copies of issue

PUBLICATION TIME LAG: Not given
PROOFS: No
PAGE CHARGES: No

ALPHABETICAL LISTING OF JOURNALS / 133

**JOURNAL TITLE:** New Library World

**SUBSCRIPTION ADDRESS:** New Library World, 16 Pembridge Road, London W11 3HL, England

**PRICE:** $30
**CIRCULATION:** 1,400
**AFFILIATION:** None
**INDEXED/ABSTRACTED:** LISA

**FREQUENCY:** Monthly

**MANUSCRIPT ADDRESS:** Clive Bingley (Journals), Ltd., 16 Pembridge Road, London W11 3HL, England

**EDITORIAL POLICY:** News, comment, current affairs in library science

**AUDIENCE:** Professional librarians

**PREFERRED TOPICS:** Various aspects of professional librarianship

**INAPPROPRIATE TOPICS:** Not given

**FEATURES:** Not given

**REVIEWS:** Yes

**STUDENT PAPERS:** No

**RESTRICTIONS:** None
**COVER LETTER:** No
**NUMBER OF COPIES:** 1
**STYLE:** No recommendation
**FORMAT:** No recommendation

**ABSTRACT:** No
**LENGTH:** 1,000-5,000
**INSTRUCTION FORM:** No

**ACKNOWLEDGED:** Not given
**REVIEW PROCESS:** Editor

**NOTIFICATION TIME:** Not given

**CRITICISM:** No

**ACCEPTANCE RATE:** Not given
**REVISION:** Varies
**EARLY PUBLICATION OPTION:** Not given
**COPYRIGHT POLICY:** Publisher
**FEE:** 10 pounds per 1,000 words
**REPRINTS:** 1

**PUBLICATION TIME LAG:** 1-2 months
**PROOFS:** No

**PAGE CHARGES:** No

JOURNAL TITLE: Notes

SUBSCRIPTION ADDRESS: Business Office, Music Library Association, 2017 Walnut Street, Philadelphia, PA 19103

PRICE: $21
CIRCULATION: 3,700
AFFILIATION: Music Library Association
INDEXED/ABSTRACTED: AHCI, BRD, BRI, GPA, LISA, LL, MAG, MuI, RILM

FREQUENCY: Quarterly

MANUSCRIPT ADDRESS: William M. McClellan, Music Library, Music Building, University of Illinois, Urbana, IL 61801

EDITORIAL POLICY: To maintain NOTES as the foremost periodical in the field of music bibliography as well as the scholarly journal of the Music Library Association

AUDIENCE: Librarians, music faculty in higher education, the music trade

PREFERRED TOPICS: Music bibliography and discography, technical problems and programs, and library-related articles concerning musicology, music printing and publishing

INAPPROPRIATE TOPICS: Analytical articles on composers' styles and specific compositions; biographical studies of musicians

FEATURES: "Classics of Music Literature," "Music Literature Indexes in Review"

REVIEWS: Yes

STUDENT PAPERS: No

RESTRICTIONS: None
COVER LETTER: Yes
NUMBER OF COPIES: 1
STYLE: Chicago
FORMAT: Standard

ABSTRACT: No
LENGTH: 5,000-10,000
INSTRUCTION FORM: Yes

ACKNOWLEDGED: Yes
REVIEW PROCESS: External reviewer

NOTIFICATION TIME: 4-6 weeks

CRITICISM: Yes

ACCEPTANCE RATE: 25%
REVISION: Medium
EARLY PUBLICATION OPTION: No
COPYRIGHT POLICY: Publisher
FEE: None
REPRINTS: 40

PUBLICATION TIME LAG: 6-24 months
PROOFS: Yes
PAGE CHARGES: No

**JOURNAL TITLE:** Occasional Papers

**SUBSCRIPTION ADDRESS:** Graduate School of Library Science Publications Office, 249 Armory Building, University of Illinois, Champaign, IL 61820

**PRICE:** $7
**FREQUENCY:** 5 x a year
**CIRCULATION:** 1,000
**AFFILIATION:** U. of Illinois Graduate School of Library Science
**INDEXED/ABSTRACTED:** CBI, LL

**MANUSCRIPT ADDRESS:** Linda Hoffman, Occasional Papers, 249 Armory Building, University of Illinois, Graduate School of Library Science, Champaign, IL 61820

**EDITORIAL POLICY:** Acceptable papers deal with some aspect of librarianship, and which, because of length, specialization, or temporary interest, would not ordinarily be published in a library periodical

**AUDIENCE:** Researchers; librarians; library students, faculty, staff

**PREFERRED TOPICS:** Specialized studies, bibliographies

**INAPPROPRIATE TOPICS:** "How to" or "How we did it" papers of narrow interest and restricted applicability

**FEATURES:** None. Each Occasional Paper consists of a single article

**REVIEWS:** No
**STUDENT PAPERS:** Yes

**RESTRICTIONS:** None
**COVER LETTER:** Yes
**NUMBER OF COPIES:** 1
**STYLE:** Chicago
**FORMAT:** Standard
**ABSTRACT LENGTH:** 100-250
**INSTRUCTION FORM:** Yes
**LENGTH:** 10,000

**ACKNOWLEDGED:** Yes
**NOTIFICATION TIME:** 3-6 weeks
**REVIEW PROCESS:** External reviewers

**CRITICISM:** Yes

**ACCEPTANCE RATE:** 50%
**REVISION:** Medium
**EARLY PUBLICATION OPTION:** No
**COPYRIGHT POLICY:** Not copyrighted
**FEE:** None
**REPRINTS:** 12 copies of issue
**PUBLICATION TIME LAG:** 15 months
**PROOFS:** No
**PAGE CHARGES:** No

**JOURNAL TITLE:** Online Magazine

**SUBSCRIPTION ADDRESS:** Online, 11 Tannery Lane, Weston, CT 06883

**PRICE:** $52
**CIRCULATION:** 3,500
**AFFILIATION:** None
**INDEXED/ABSTRACTED:** CIJE, INSPEC, LISA, MI
**FREQUENCY:** Quarterly

**MANUSCRIPT ADDRESS:** Barbara A. Marshall, Online, 11 Tannery Lane, Weston, CT 06883

**EDITORIAL POLICY:** Covers entire field of online information: databases, search techniques, management, new applications, reviews, news pages, and special columns
**AUDIENCE:** Librarians and information managers
**PREFERRED TOPICS:** Research and review articles in the field of online information
**INAPPROPRIATE TOPICS:** Theoretical and philosophical articles

**FEATURES:** None

**REVIEWS:** Yes
**STUDENT PAPERS:** No

**RESTRICTIONS:** None
**COVER LETTER:** Yes
**NUMBER OF COPIES:** 3
**STYLE:** House
**FORMAT:** Standard
**ABSTRACT:** No
**LENGTH:** 500-3,000
**INSTRUCTION FORM:** Yes

**ACKNOWLEDGED:** Yes
**REVIEW PROCESS:** External reviewers
**NOTIFICATION TIME:** 1-2 months

**CRITICISM:** Usually

**ACCEPTANCE RATE:** 65%
**REVISION:** Medium
**EARLY PUBLICATION OPTION:** No
**COPYRIGHT POLICY:** Publisher
**FEE:** $50-$100 after publication
**REPRINTS:** 20
**PUBLICATION TIME LAG:** 3-4 months
**PROOFS:** Yes
**PAGE CHARGES:** No

**JOURNAL TITLE:** Online Review

**SUBSCRIPTION ADDRESS:** Thomas H. Hogan, Box 550, Marlton, NJ 08053

**PRICE:** $30
**CIRCULATION:** Not given
**AFFILIATION:** None
**INDEXED/ABSTRACTED:** ISA, LISA

**FREQUENCY:** Quarterly

**MANUSCRIPT ADDRESS:** Martha E. Williams, Online Review, RR No. 1, Monticello, IL 61856

**EDITORIAL POLICY:** Publication of articles, features and news monitoring the online information industry.

**AUDIENCE:** Online professionals, users, librarians

**PREFERRED TOPICS:** Online information research, development, and activities and related products

**INAPPROPRIATE TOPICS:** Not given

**FEATURES:** News Section

**REVIEWS:** Yes

**STUDENT PAPERS:** No

**RESTRICTIONS:** None
**COVER LETTER:** Yes
**NUMBER OF COPIES:** 2
**STYLE:** House
**FORMAT:** Standard

**ABSTRACT:** 100
**LENGTH:** 3,000-5,000
**INSTRUCTION FORM:** House

**ACKNOWLEDGED:** Yes
**REVIEW PROCESS:** Editorial board

**NOTIFICATION TIME:** 3-6 months

**CRITICISM:** Yes

**ACCEPTANCE RATE:** 50%
**REVISION:** Light
**EARLY PUBLICATION OPTION:** No
**COPYRIGHT POLICY:** Publisher
**FEE:** None
**REPRINTS:** 30

**PUBLICATION TIME LAG:** 3-6 months
**PROOFS:** Yes

**PAGE CHARGES:** No

**JOURNAL TITLE:** Outlook on Research Libraries
**SUBSCRIPTION ADDRESS:** Elsevier Sequoia S.A., P. O. Box 851, Lausanne, Switzerland

**PRICE:** $70
**CIRCULATION:** Not given
**AFFILIATION:** None
**INDEXED/ABSTRACTED:** LL
**FREQUENCY:** Monthly

**MANUSCRIPT ADDRESS:** Elsevier's Science Division, P.O. Box 2400, Jan van Galenstraat 335, 100 AW Amsterdam, Netherlands
**EDITORIAL POLICY:** Monthly provision of news and review service, highlighting current trends and developments affecting research library management and operations
**AUDIENCE:** Academic and research librarians, library suppliers, publishers, etc.
**PREFERRED TOPICS:** Trends and developments affecting research library management and operations

**INAPPROPRIATE TOPICS:** Scholarly articles

**FEATURES:** News or review items from geographical areas infrequently covered in the literature

**REVIEWS:** No
**STUDENT PAPERS:** Not given

**RESTRICTIONS:** Not given
**COVER LETTER:** Not given
**NUMBER OF COPIES:** Not given
**STYLE:** Not given
**FORMAT:** Standard
**ABSTRACT:** No
**LENGTH:** 500
**INSTRUCTION FORM:** No

**ACKNOWLEDGED:** Yes
**REVIEW PROCESS:** Editorial board
**NOTIFICATION TIME:** 1 month

**CRITICISM:** No

**ACCEPTANCE RATE:** Not given
**REVISION:** Medium
**EARLY PUBLICATION OPTION:** No
**COPYRIGHT POLICY:** Publisher
**FEE:** $50-$100 on publication
**REPRINTS:** Reasonable requests met
**PUBLICATION TIME LAG:** 1 month
**PROOFS:** No
**PAGE CHARGES:** No

**JOURNAL TITLE:** PNLA Quarterly

**SUBSCRIPTION ADDRESS:** PNLA Quarterly, Portland State University, P.O. Box 1151, Portland, OR 97207

**PRICE:** $10
**CIRCULATION:** 1,300
**AFFILIATION:** Pacific Northwest Library Association
**INDEXED/ABSTRACTED:** LISA, LL
**FREQUENCY:** Quarterly

**MANUSCRIPT ADDRESS:** Daniel Newberry, Portland State Unive-sity, P.O. Box 1151, Portland, OR 97207

**EDITORIAL POLICY:** As the official organ of the Pacific Northwest Library Association publishes articles, book reviews and bibliographies pertinent to Northwest libraries
**AUDIENCE:** Members of PNLA and the professional library community of the Northwest
**PREFERRED TOPICS:** Those pertinent to Northwest libraries

**INAPPROPRIATE TOPICS:** Professional general interest topics (frequently library school papers)

**FEATURES:** Annual bibliography of Northwestiana

**REVIEWS:** Yes
**STUDENT PAPERS:** No

**RESTRICTIONS:** None
**COVER LETTER:** Yes
**NUMBER OF COPIES:** 5
**STYLE:** Chicago
**FORMAT:** Standard
**ABSTRACT:** No
**LENGTH:** 2,000
**INSTRUCTION FORM:** Yes

**ACKNOWLEDGED:** Yes
**REVIEW PROCESS:** Editorial board
**NOTIFICATION TIME:** 1 month

**CRITICISM:** Sometimes

**ACCEPTANCE RATE:** 50%
**REVISION:** Medium
**EARLY PUBLICATION OPTION:** No
**COPYRIGHT POLICY:** Author
**FEE:** None
**REPRINTS:** None
**PUBLICATION TIME LAG:** 3-6 months
**PROOFS:** No
**PAGE CHARGES:** No

**JOURNAL TITLE:** Phaedrus

**SUBSCRIPTION ADDRESS:** K. G. Saur Publishing, 45 North Broad St., Ridgewood, NJ 07450

**PRICE:** $18
**CIRCULATION:** 650
**AFFILIATION:** None
**INDEXED/ABSTRACTED:** BKJ, CLA, IRB, MLA, PH

**FREQUENCY:** 3 x a year

**MANUSCRIPT ADDRESS:** James Fraser, Phaedrus, Fairleigh Dickinson University, Madison, NJ 07940

**EDITORIAL POLICY:** To provide researchers in children's literature with bibliographical notes and reviews of inquiry into the media environment of the child

**AUDIENCE:** Social scientists, literary historians, psychologists, editors, pedagogues, librarians

**PREFERRED TOPICS:** Periodical, book, school book, comic book, song book, boxed game, film, television, and oral literature directed to the child

**INAPPROPRIATE TOPICS:** Reading research and library service to the child; no unsolicited manuscripts are accepted

**FEATURES:** None

**REVIEWS:** Yes

**STUDENT PAPERS:** Yes

**RESTRICTIONS:** None
**COVER LETTER:** No
**NUMBER OF COPIES:** Not given
**STYLE:** Chicago
**FORMAT:** Standard

**ABSTRACT:** No
**LENGTH:** Not given
**INSTRUCTION FORM:** Yes

**ACKNOWLEDGED:** Yes
**REVIEW PROCESS:** Editorial board

**NOTIFICATION TIME:** Not given

**CRITICISM:** Yes

**ACCEPTANCE RATE:** Solicited only
**REVISION:** Varies
**EARLY PUBLICATION OPTION:** No
**COPYRIGHT POLICY:** Author
**FEE:** Sometimes
**REPRINTS:** 3 copies of issue

**PUBLICATION TIME LAG:** Not given
**PROOFS:** Yes
**PAGE CHARGES:** No

JOURNAL TITLE: Private Library

SUBSCRIPTION ADDRESS: Private Libraries Association, c/o Hon. Publications Secretary, David Chambers, Ravelston, South View Road, Pinner, Middlesex, England

PRICE: $24
CIRCULATION: 1,250
AFFILIATION: Private Libraries Association
INDEXED/ABSTRACTED: LISA, LL
FREQUENCY: Quarterly

MANUSCRIPT ADDRESS: John Cotton, Private Library, Private Libraries Association, Ravelston, South View Road, Pinner, Middlesex, England

EDITORIAL POLICY: Articles on book collecting, with particular stress on the work of private presses, both in England and abroad

AUDIENCE: Members of the Private Libraries Association

PREFERRED TOPICS: Book collecting; book illustrators; private presses; bookbinding; book plates

INAPPROPRIATE TOPICS: Not given

FEATURES: An annual checklist of titles, Private Press books

REVIEWS: Yes
STUDENT PAPERS: No

RESTRICTIONS: None
COVER LETTER: Yes
NUMBER OF COPIES: 1
STYLE: No recommendations
FORMAT: Standard
ABSTRACT: No
LENGTH: 2,000-4,000
INSTRUCTION FORM: No

ACKNOWLEDGED: Yes
REVIEW PROCESS: Editor
NOTIFICATION TIME: 1 month

CRITICISM: No

ACCEPTANCE RATE: 50%
REVISION: Medium to light
EARLY PUBLICATION OPTION: No
COPYRIGHT POLICY: Author and publisher
FEE: 25 pounds
REPRINTS: 24 copies of issue
PUBLICATION TIME LAG: 6 months
PROOFS: Yes
PAGE CHARGES: No

JOURNAL TITLE: Program

SUBSCRIPTION ADDRESS: Publications (Sales) Department, Aslib, 3 Belgrave Square, London SW1X 8PL England

PRICE: $34.50
CIRCULATION: 1,500
AFFILIATION: Aslib
INDEXED/ABSTRACTED: CC, INSPEC, LISA, LL, SA, SSCI

FREQUENCY: Quarterly

MANUSCRIPT ADDRESS: John Eyre, Program, Polytechnic of North London, School of Librarianship, 207-225 Essex Road, London N1 3PN, England

EDITORIAL POLICY: Devoted to all aspects of the use of computers in library and information services

AUDIENCE: Members of Aslib and professional librarians

PREFERRED TOPICS: Automated library and information systems, technical developments of networks, microcomputers

INAPPROPRIATE TOPICS: Not given

FEATURES: Not given

REVIEWS: Yes

STUDENT PAPERS: No

RESTRICTIONS: None
COVER LETTER: Yes
NUMBER OF COPIES: 2
STYLE: No recommendation
FORMAT: No recommendation

ABSTRACT: 300
LENGTH: 4,000
INSTRUCTION FORM: see journal

ACKNOWLEDGED: Yes
REVIEW PROCESS: Editorial board and external reviewers

NOTIFICATION TIME: 2 months

CRITICISM: Yes

ACCEPTANCE RATE: 80%
REVISION: Light
EARLY PUBLICATION OPTION: No
COPYRIGHT POLICY: Author
FEE: None
REPRINTS: 25

PUBLICATION TIME LAG: 6-9 months
PROOFS: Yes

PAGE CHARGES: No

**JOURNAL TITLE:** Public Libraries

**SUBSCRIPTION ADDRESS:** Public Library Association, 50 E. Huron Street, Chicago, IL 60611

**PRICE:** $10
**FREQUENCY:** Quarterly
**CIRCULATION:** 5,000
**AFFILIATION:** Public Library Association
**INDEXED/ABSTRACTED:** CALL, LL

**MANUSCRIPT ADDRESS:** Kenneth Shearer, Public Libraries, School of Library Science, North Carolina Central University, Durham, NC 27707

**EDITORIAL POLICY:** To further the mission and work of the PLA membership; to serve the interests of public libraries and public librarianship in the U.S.

**AUDIENCE:** Public Library Association members, and others concerned with public librarianship

**PREFERRED TOPICS:** Socio-economic context of libraries; surveys of public libraries, librarians; librarianship; research findings with clear implications for the profession; think/opinion pieces

**INAPPROPRIATE TOPICS:** Those not clearly related to public libraries

**FEATURES:** At Our Place; Etcetera; Service to children; Public Laws/Public Libraries; Research in Action; ERIC Documents of Note; In Review

**REVIEWS:** Yes
**STUDENT PAPERS:** No

**RESTRICTIONS:** None
**COVER LETTER:** Yes
**NUMBER OF COPIES:** 2
**STYLE:** House
**FORMAT:** House
**ABSTRACT:** No
**LENGTH:** 1,500
**INSTRUCTION FORM:** No

**ACKNOWLEDGED:** Yes
**REVIEW PROCESS:** Editor
**NOTIFICATION TIME:** 3 months

**CRITICISM:** If possible

**ACCEPTANCE RATE:** 30%
**REVISION:** Light
**EARLY PUBLICATION OPTION:** No
**COPYRIGHT POLICY:** Publisher
**FEE:** None
**REPRINTS:** None
**PUBLICATION TIME LAG:** 3-5 months
**PROOFS:** No
**PAGE CHARGES:** No

JOURNAL TITLE: Public Library Quarterly

SUBSCRIPTION ADDRESS: Haworth Press, 28 East 22 Street, New York, NY 10010

PRICE: $30
CIRCULATION: 1,000
AFFILIATION: None
INDEXED/ABSTRACTED: LL

FREQUENCY: Quarterly

MANUSCRIPT ADDRESS: Richard Waters, Public Library Quarterly, 1954 Commerce Street, Dallas, TX 75212

EDITORIAL POLICY: Will provide fresh, creative and scholarly papers devoted to critical and current topics

AUDIENCE: Public library administrators, practitioners, trustees, etc.

PREFERRED TOPICS: Those that extend, explain, clarify our knowledge of the purposes and possibilities of the public library

INAPPROPRIATE TOPICS: How we do it good in . . .

FEATURES: Public library in context

REVIEWS: Yes

STUDENT PAPERS: Yes

RESTRICTIONS: None
COVER LETTER: Yes
NUMBER OF COPIES: 3
STYLE: Chicago
FORMAT: Standard

ABSTRACT: 100
LENGTH: 3,500-4,000
INSTRUCTION FORM: Yes

ACKNOWLEDGED: Yes (SASE)
REVIEW PROCESS: Editorial board

NOTIFICATION TIME: 6 weeks

CRITICISM: Yes

ACCEPTANCE RATE: 50%
REVISION: Light
EARLY PUBLICATION OPTION: Yes
COPYRIGHT POLICY: Publisher
FEE: None
REPRINTS: 10

PUBLICATION TIME LAG: Up to 6 months
PROOFS: Yes
PAGE CHARGES: No

**JOURNAL TITLE:** RQ

**SUBSCRIPTION ADDRESS:** American Library Association, 50 E. Huron Street, Chicago, IL 60611

**PRICE:** $20
**FREQUENCY:** Quarterly
**CIRCULATION:** 6,000
**AFFILIATION:** ALA Reference and Adult Services Division
**INDEXED/ABSTRACTED:** BRI, CIJE, ISA, LISA, LL

**MANUSCRIPT ADDRESS:** Helen B. Josephine, RQ, P.O. Box 246, Berkeley, CA 94701

**EDITORIAL POLICY:** To disseminate materials of interest to reference librarians, bibliographers, adult services librarians, and others interested in user-oriented library services
**AUDIENCE:** Members of the Reference and Adult Services Division of ALA
**PREFERRED TOPICS:** Organization and management of reference departments, uses of reference tools, reference service policy, online reference, library instruction
**INAPPROPRIATE TOPICS:** Not given

**FEATURES:** Notes from RASD Headquarters; The Exchange; Backtalk; ILL Issues, LC News

**REVIEWS:** Yes
**STUDENT PAPERS:** No

**RESTRICTIONS:** None
**COVER LETTER:** Yes
**NUMBER OF COPIES:** 2
**STYLE:** Chicago
**FORMAT:** Standard
**ABSTRACT:** 100
**LENGTH:** Varies
**INSTRUCTION FORM:** Yes

**ACKNOWLEDGED:** Yes
**REVIEW PROCESS:** Not given
**NOTIFICATION TIME:** 3 months

**CRITICISM:** Sometimes

**ACCEPTANCE RATE:** 25-30%
**REVISION:** Light
**EARLY PUBLICATION OPTION:** No
**COPYRIGHT POLICY:** Publisher
**FEE:** None
**REPRINTS:** 1 copy of issue
**PUBLICATION TIME LAG:** 6 months
**PROOFS:** Yes
**PAGE CHARGES:** No

**JOURNAL TITLE:** RTSD Newsletter

**SUBSCRIPTION ADDRESS:** American Library Association--RTSD, 50 E. Huron Street, Chicago, IL 60611

**PRICE:** Free with membership
**FREQUENCY:** 6 x a year
**CIRCULATION:** 9,000
**AFFILIATION:** ALA Resources and Technical Services Division
**INDEXED/ABSTRACTED:** Not

**MANUSCRIPT ADDRESS:** Arnold Hirshon, Box 9184 Duke Station, Durham, NC 27706

**EDITORIAL POLICY:** Articles are printed which concern cataloging, classification, acquisitions, collection development, preservation, reprography, etc. of all types of library materials
**AUDIENCE:** Resources and Technical Services Division membership
**PREFERRED TOPICS:** Those which concern themselves with any phase of library resources and technical services

**INAPPROPRIATE TOPICS:** Not given

**FEATURES:** State of the art articles on areas of interest to the membership

**REVIEWS:** Yes
**STUDENT PAPERS:** No

**RESTRICTIONS:** None
**COVER LETTER:** Yes
**NUMBER OF COPIES:** 1
**STYLE:** Chicago
**FORMAT:** Standard
**ABSTRACT:** No
**LENGTH:** Up to 1,750
**INSTRUCTION FORM:** Yes

**ACKNOWLEDGED:** Yes
**REVIEW PROCESS:** Editor
**NOTIFICATION TIME:** 1-2 months

**CRITICISM:** Yes

**ACCEPTANCE RATE:** Unknown
**REVISION:** Medium
**EARLY PUBLICATION OPTION:** No
**COPYRIGHT POLICY:** Publisher
**FEE:** None
**REPRINTS:** Negotiable
**PUBLICATION TIME LAG:** Up to 6 months
**PROOFS:** No
**PAGE CHARGES:** No

JOURNAL TITLE: Reference Book Review

SUBSCRIPTION ADDRESS: Reference Book Review, P.O. Box 19954, Dallas, TX 75219

PRICE: $11
CIRCULATION: 1,000
AFFILIATION: None
INDEXED/ABSTRACTED: Not

FREQUENCY: Quarterly

MANUSCRIPT ADDRESS: Cameron Northouse, Reference Book Review, P.O. Box 19954, Dallas, TX 75219

EDITORIAL POLICY: Approximately 100 reviews per issue of current reference books in all fields

AUDIENCE: Acquisitions and reference librarians

PREFERRED TOPICS: Reviews only

INAPPROPRIATE TOPICS: Articles of any kind

FEATURES: Not given

REVIEWS: Yes

STUDENT PAPERS: No

RESTRICTIONS: Not given
COVER LETTER: Yes
NUMBER OF COPIES: 1
STYLE: House
FORMAT: Standard

ABSTRACT: No
LENGTH: 300-500
INSTRUCTION FORM:

ACKNOWLEDGED: Yes
REVIEW PROCESS: Editorial board

NOTIFICATION TIME: 1 week

CRITICISM: No

ACCEPTANCE RATE: 50%
REVISION: Light
EARLY PUBLICATION OPTION: No
COPYRIGHT POLICY: Publisher
FEE: None
REPRINTS: 5

PUBLICATION TIME LAG: 1-2 months
PROOFS: No
PAGE CHARGES: No

**JOURNAL TITLE:** Reference Services Review
**SUBSCRIPTION ADDRESS:** Pierian Press, P.O. Box 1808, Ann Arbor, MI 48106

**PRICE:** $25
**CIRCULATION:** 1,500
**AFFILIATION:** No
**INDEXED/ABSTRACTED:** BRI, CALL, LL
**FREQUENCY:** Quarterly

**MANUSCRIPT ADDRESS:** Cecily Johns, RSR, 2570 Madison Road #10, Cincinnati, OH 45208

**EDITORIAL POLICY:** Devoted to reviewing and evaluating a wide variety of publications having reference value within general, academic, and special library settings.
**AUDIENCE:** Reference and collection development librarians
**PREFERRED TOPICS:** Bibliographic essays which survey current trends in reference works; essays which survey significant reference sources in a particular subject area or genre.
**INAPPROPRIATE TOPICS:** Unannotated bibliographies of reference sources or professional sources with a brief introduction
**FEATURES:** The Reference Interview; An Annotated Bibliography

**REVIEWS:** Yes
**STUDENT PAPERS:** No

**RESTRICTIONS:** None
**COVER LETTER:** Yes
**NUMBER OF COPIES:** 1
**STYLE:** Chicago
**FORMAT:** Standard
**ABSTRACT:** No
**LENGTH:** 2,500
**INSTRUCTION FORM:** Yes

**ACKNOWLEDGED:** Yes
**REVIEW PROCESS:** Review by column or feature editor
**NOTIFICATION TIME:** 1 month

**CRITICISM:** No

**ACCEPTANCE RATE:** 90%
**REVISION:** Medium
**EARLY PUBLICATION OPTION:** No
**COPYRIGHT POLICY:** Publisher
**FEE:** None
**REPRINTS:** None
**PUBLICATION TIME LAG:** 6 months
**PROOFS:** No
**PAGE CHARGES:** No

JOURNAL TITLE: Reprographics Quarterly

SUBSCRIPTION ADDRESS: The National Reprographic Centre, Bayfordbury, Hertford, Hertfordshire SG13 8LD, England

PRICE: $40
CIRCULATION: 1,000
AFFILIATION: None
INDEXED/ABSTRACTED: LISA, LL

FREQUENCY: Quarterly

MANUSCRIPT ADDRESS: B. J. S. Williams, Reprographics Quarterly, National Reprographic Centre for Documentation, Endymion Road, Hatfield, Hertfordshire AL10 8Au, England
EDITORIAL POLICY: Deals with the applications and technology of micrographic, reprographic, word processing and other new media for documentation.
AUDIENCE: Reprographic managers, librarians, information scientists, manufacturers in the field
PREFERRED TOPICS: Research findings in areas of micrographics

INAPPROPRIATE TOPICS: Not given

FEATURES: Not given

REVIEWS: Solicited only        STUDENT PAPERS: No

RESTRICTIONS: None
COVER LETTER: Yes
NUMBER OF COPIES: Not given
STYLE: No recommendation
FORMAT: No recommendation

ABSTRACT: 100
LENGTH: 5,000-6,000
INSTRUCTION FORM: Not given

ACKNOWLEDGED: Yes
REVIEW PROCESS: Editorial board and external reviewers
CRITICISM: No

NOTIFICATION TIME: 1 month

ACCEPTANCE RATE: 70%
REVISION: Light
EARLY PUBLICATION OPTION: No
COPYRIGHT POLICY: Publisher
FEE: None
REPRINTS: 6

PUBLICATION TIME LAG: 6 months
PROOFS: If required
PAGE CHARGES: No

JOURNAL TITLE: Resource Sharing & Library Networks

SUBSCRIPTION ADDRESS: Haworth Press, 28 East 22 Street, New York, NY 10010

PRICE: $35
CIRCULATION: Not given (new journal)
AFFILIATION: None
INDEXED/ABSTRACTED: Not

FREQUENCY: Quarterly

MANUSCRIPT ADDRESS: Ward Shaw, Resource Sharing & Library Networks, Denver Public Library, 3840 York, Denver, CO 80205

EDITORIAL POLICY: To provide an international forum for the exchange of information about the rapidly developing field of network development and cooperation.

AUDIENCE: The library and information community

PREFERRED TOPICS: Librarianship, information science, computer science, management, operations research, economics, the behavioral sciences, and political science.

INAPPROPRIATE TOPICS: Not given

FEATURES: Not given

REVIEWS: Not given

STUDENT PAPERS: Yes

RESTRICTIONS: None
COVER LETTER: Yes
NUMBER OF COPIES: 3
STYLE: Chicago
FORMAT: Standard

ABSTRACT: 100
LENGTH: 12-24 pages
INSTRUCTION FORM:

ACKNOWLEDGED: Yes (SASE)
REVIEW PROCESS: Editorial board and external reviewers

NOTIFICATION TIME: Not given

CRITICISM: Yes

ACCEPTANCE RATE: Not given
REVISION: Not given
EARLY PUBLICATION OPTION: Yes
COPYRIGHT POLICY: Publisher
FEE: None
REPRINTS: 10

PUBLICATION TIME LAG: Not given
PROOFS: Yes
PAGE CHARGES: Yes, if early publication

JOURNAL TITLE: SRRT Newsletter

SUBSCRIPTION ADDRESS: ALA/SRRT Clearinghouse, 6 Jones Street, #24, New York, NY 10014

PRICE: $5
CIRCULATION: 1,000
AFFILIATION: ALA Social Responsibilities Round Table
INDEXED/ABSTRACTED: Not given
FREQUENCY: Irregular

MANUSCRIPT ADDRESS: Julie McCartney, ALA/SRRT Clearinghouse, 6 Jones Street, #24, New York, NY 10014

EDITORIAL POLICY: Published in order to provide communication between the various members and task forces of SRRT

AUDIENCE: Librarians, library staffers

PREFERRED TOPICS: Material that relates to social concerns of librarians

INAPPROPRIATE TOPICS: Not given

FEATURES: Lists of out of the way publications; news on task forces of SRRT

REVIEWS: No          STUDENT PAPERS: Yes

RESTRICTIONS: None
COVER LETTER: Yes
NUMBER OF COPIES: 1
STYLE: No recommendation
FORMAT: No recommendation
ABSTRACT: No
LENGTH: 700-1,000
INSTRUCTION FORM: No

ACKNOWLEDGED: Yes
REVIEW PROCESS: Editorial board
NOTIFICATION TIME: 3 weeks

CRITICISM: Yes

ACCEPTANCE RATE: 90%
REVISION: Light
EARLY PUBLICATION OPTION: No
COPYRIGHT POLICY: Not copyrighted
FEE: None
REPRINTS: Up to 10, upon request
PUBLICATION TIME LAG: 6 months
PROOFS: No
PAGE CHARGES: No

**JOURNAL TITLE:** The School Librarian

**SUBSCRIPTION ADDRESS:** School Library Association, Victoria House, 29-31 George Street, Oxford OX1 1AY, England

**PRICE:** $30

**FREQUENCY:** Quarterly

**CIRCULATION:** 6,000

**AFFILIATION:** The School Library Association

**INDEXED/ABSTRACTED:** BEI, LISA, LL

**MANUSCRIPT ADDRESS:** Walter Ovens, 82 Woodland Avenue, Kidderminster DY11 5AN, England

**EDITORIAL POLICY:** Articles about administration and organization of school libraries, reviews of books and other teaching materials

**AUDIENCE:** Teachers and librarians

**PREFERRED TOPICS:** Articles on authors of children's books; book reviews; theories of information retrieval and dissemination; awareness of new trends and use of new technology.

**INAPPROPRIATE TOPICS:** Carelessly written and presented copy or articles which are verbose

**FEATURES:** Monographs of writers of children's books, annotated lists of subject books

**REVIEWS:** Yes

**STUDENT PAPERS:** Yes

**RESTRICTIONS:** None
**COVER LETTER:** Yes
**NUMBER OF COPIES:** 2
**STYLE:** House
**FORMAT:** Standard

**ABSTRACT:** No
**LENGTH:** 3,200
**INSTRUCTION FORM:** Yes

**ACKNOWLEDGED:** Yes
**REVIEW PROCESS:** Editor

**NOTIFICATION TIME:** 4-6 weeks

**CRITICISM:** Yes

**ACCEPTANCE RATE:** 80%
**REVISION:** Medium
**EARLY PUBLICATION OPTION:** Not given
**COPYRIGHT POLICY:** Publisher
**FEE:** $2 per page upon publication
**REPRINTS:** 1 copy of issue

**PUBLICATION TIME LAG:** 1-6 months
**PROOFS:** Yes
**PAGE CHARGES:** Not given

**JOURNAL TITLE:** School Library Journal

**SUBSCRIPTION ADDRESS:** R. R. Bowker Company, Subscription Department, P.O. Box 67, Whitinsville, MA 01588

**PRICE:** $20
**CIRCULATION:** 44,000
**AFFILIATION:** No
**INDEXED/ABSTRACTED:** ARG, BRD, LISA, LL

**FREQUENCY:** 9 x a year

**MANUSCRIPT ADDRESS:** Lillian N. Gerhardt, School Library Journal, R. R. Bowker Company, 1180 Avenue of the Americas, New York, NY 10036

**EDITORIAL POLICY:** Articles on books and library services for children and young adults in schools and public libraries.

**AUDIENCE:** Librarians serving children and young adults in schools and public libraries

**PREFERRED TOPICS:** Critical articles on books and non-print materials, and issues in library service to children and young adults.

**INAPPROPRIATE TOPICS:** Head-counting of racial/sex/ethnic stereotypes in books for children

**FEATURES:** Monthly columns with different authors: "Make Your Point," "Practically Speaking," and "In the YA Corner"

**REVIEWS:** Yes   **STUDENT PAPERS:** Yes

**RESTRICTIONS:** No
**COVER LETTER:** Yes
**NUMBER OF COPIES:** 1
**STYLE:** No recommendation
**FORMAT:** Standard

**ABSTRACT:** No
**LENGTH:** 3,500-4,000
**INSTRUCTION FORM:** Yes

**ACKNOWLEDGED:** Yes
**REVIEW PROCESS:** Editors

**NOTIFICATION TIME:** 3-4 months

**CRITICISM:** No

**ACCEPTANCE RATE:** 15%
**REVISION:** Medium
**EARLY PUBLICATION OPTION:** No
**COPYRIGHT POLICY:** Assigned to author on request
**FEE:** $100 on publication
**REPRINTS:** 2-8 copies of issue

**PUBLICATION TIME LAG:** 2 months
**PROOFS:** No
**PAGE CHARGES:** No

JOURNAL TITLE: Science & Technology Libraries

SUBSCRIPTION ADDRESS: Haworth Press, 28 East 22 Street, New York, NY 10010

PRICE: $42
CIRCULATION: Not given (new journal)
AFFILIATION: None
INDEXED/ABSTRACTED: Not

FREQUENCY: Quarterly

MANUSCRIPT ADDRESS: Ellis Mount, Science & Technology Libraries, School of Library Service, Columbia University, Butler Library, New York, NY 10027

EDITORIAL POLICY: To discuss topics relevant to the management, operation, collections, services and staffing of all types of libraries in the science and technology field

AUDIENCE: Sci-tech librarians and information center staffs

PREFERRED TOPICS: Primarily those matching the themes of the issues, but will consider longer research treatises or tutorial papers

INAPPROPRIATE TOPICS: Not given

FEATURES: Articles related to the theme of each issue

REVIEWS: Yes

STUDENT PAPERS: No

RESTRICTIONS: None
COVER LETTER: Yes
NUMBER OF COPIES: 3
STYLE: Chicago
FORMAT: Standard

ABSTRACT: No
LENGTH: 12-25 pages
INSTRUCTION FORM: Yes

ACKNOWLEDGED: Yes (SASE)
REVIEW PROCESS: External reviewers

NOTIFICATION TIME: 3 weeks

CRITICISM: Not usually

ACCEPTANCE RATE: Not yet known
REVISION: Medium
EARLY PUBLICATION OPTION: Yes
COPYRIGHT POLICY: Publisher
FEE: None
REPRINTS: 10

PUBLICATION TIME LAG: Not given
PROOFS: Yes

PAGE CHARGES: Only with early publication option

**JOURNAL TITLE:** Serials Librarian

**SUBSCRIPTION ADDRESS:** Haworth Press, 28 East 22 Street, New York, NY 10010

**PRICE:** $40
**CIRCULATION:** 1,400
**AFFILIATION:** No
**INDEXED/ABSTRACTED:** AHL, BS101, CALL, CC, LISA, LL, SSCI

**FREQUENCY:** Quarterly

**MANUSCRIPT ADDRESS:** Peter Gellatly, Serials Librarian, 310 Third Street, New Westminster, BC, Canada V3L 2R9

**EDITORIAL POLICY:** Articles on all aspects of serials librarianship in all types of libraries.

**AUDIENCE:** Librarians, publishers and subscription agencies

**PREFERRED TOPICS:** Serials management, serials cataloging and automation, collection measurement and evaluation, collection development, copyright, periodicals history

**INAPPROPRIATE TOPICS:** Not given

**FEATURES:** "Into the Hopper" (government serials); "Microserials Management"; working papers on serials; Third Claim (occasional notes from publishers and agents)

**REVIEWS:** Yes
**STUDENT PAPERS:** Yes

**RESTRICTIONS:** None
**COVER LETTER:** Yes
**NUMBER OF COPIES:** 3
**STYLE:** Chicago
**FORMAT:** Standard
**ABSTRACT:** 100
**LENGTH:** 1,500-3,500
**INSTRUCTION FORM:** Yes

**ACKNOWLEDGED:** Yes (SASE)
**REVIEW PROCESS:** Editorial board and external reviewers
**NOTIFICATION TIME:** 2-8 weeks

**CRITICISM:** Yes

**ACCEPTANCE RATE:** Not given
**REVISION:** Light
**EARLY PUBLICATION OPTION:** Yes
**COPYRIGHT POLICY:** Publisher
**FEE:** None
**REPRINTS:** 10
**PUBLICATION TIME LAG:** 6-12 months
**PROOFS:** Yes
**PAGE CHARGES:** No

JOURNAL TITLE: Serials Review

SUBSCRIPTION ADDRESS: Pierian Press, P.O. Box 1808, Ann Arbor, MI 48106

PRICE: $25
CIRCULATION: 1,000
AFFILIATION: None
INDEXED/ABSTRACTED: Not given

FREQUENCY: Quarterly

MANUSCRIPT ADDRESS: Nancy Jean Nelson, P.O. Box 1808, Ann Arbor, MI 48106

EDITORIAL POLICY: To provide evaluations of periodicals, newspapers, indexes, union lists, periodical bibliographies, and other reviewing tools

AUDIENCE: Academic, public, and school librarians

PREFERRED TOPICS: Periodical selection and evaluation, development of serials budgets, copyright and interlibrary loan matters, curriculum orientation, serials automation, union listing, bibliometrics

INAPPROPRIATE TOPICS: Not given

FEATURES: Regional surveys, issues on a particular theme

REVIEWS: Yes

STUDENT PAPERS: No

RESTRICTIONS: None
COVER LETTER: Yes
NUMBER OF COPIES: 1
STYLE: Chicago
FORMAT: Standard

ABSTRACT: No
LENGTH: 1,200-3,000
INSTRUCTION FORM: Yes

ACKNOWLEDGED: Yes
REVIEW PROCESS: External reviewers

NOTIFICATION TIME: 2 months

CRITICISM: Yes

ACCEPTANCE RATE: 90%
REVISION: Light
EARLY PUBLICATION OPTION: Not given
COPYRIGHT POLICY: Publisher
FEE: None
REPRINTS: 2

PUBLICATION TIME LAG: 4-9 months
PROOFS: No
PAGE CHARGES: No

**JOURNAL TITLE:** Sightlines

**SUBSCRIPTION ADDRESS:** Educational Film Library Association, Inc., 43 West 61st Street, New York, NY 10023

**PRICE:** $25
**CIRCULATION:** 2,000
**AFFILIATION:** Educational Film Library Association
**INDEXED/ABSTRACTED:** FLI, LL, MRD
**FREQUENCY:** Quarterly

**MANUSCRIPT ADDRESS:** Nadine Covert, Sightlines, Educational Film Library Association, Inc., 43 West 61st Street, New York, NY 10023

**EDITORIAL POLICY:** Quality articles (mostly solicited) on the production and use of 16mm non-theatrical film and video in libraries, schools, museums, and communities.

**AUDIENCE:** Film librarians, film teachers in public schools, colleges, and universities, media directors

**PREFERRED TOPICS:** News of 16mm and video production, use, programming and review

**INAPPROPRIATE TOPICS:** Feature films or TV programming

**FEATURES:** "Who's Who in Filmmaking" (interview with filmmaker)

**REVIEWS:** Yes
**STUDENT PAPERS:** No

**RESTRICTIONS:** No
**COVER LETTER:** Yes
**NUMBER OF COPIES:** 2
**STYLE:** House
**FORMAT:** Standard
**ABSTRACT:** No
**LENGTH:** 1,250-1,450
**INSTRUCTION FORM:** Yes

**ACKNOWLEDGED:** Yes (SASE)
**REVIEW PROCESS:** Editors
**NOTIFICATION TIME:** 1-2 months

**CRITICISM:** Sometimes

**ACCEPTANCE RATE:** 90% solicited; 5% other
**REVISION:** Varies
**EARLY PUBLICATION OPTION:** No
**COPYRIGHT POLICY:** Author or publisher
**FEE:** $.025 per word upon publication
**REPRINTS:** 3 copies of issue
**PUBLICATION TIME LAG:** Varies
**PROOFS:** If requested
**PAGE CHARGES:** No

**JOURNAL TITLE:** Signal

**SUBSCRIPTION ADDRESS:** Thimble Press, Lockwood Station Road, South Woodchester, Gloucester GL5 5EQ, England

**PRICE:** $10
**CIRCULATION:** 1,000
**AFFILIATION:** None
**INDEXED/ABSTRACTED:** CLA

**FREQUENCY:** 3 x a year

**MANUSCRIPT ADDRESS:** Nancy Chambers, Signal, Thimble Press, Lockwood Station Road, Wouth Woodchester, Gloucester GL5 5EQ, England

**EDITORIAL POLICY:** To reflect the world of children's books from a wide range of viewpoints; to encourage the forming of a body of critical writing and thinking about children's literature

**AUDIENCE:** Individuals with more than a passing interest in the subject

**PREFERRED TOPICS:** Critical appreciations of author and illustrators, and of individual books; discussions of trends and issues within the field

**INAPPROPRIATE TOPICS:** Perfunctory pieces on 19th century children's books

**FEATURES:** Reprints articles from other sources, which are historically valuable and of special interest to scholars and researchers

**REVIEWS:** Yes
**STUDENT PAPERS:** No

**RESTRICTIONS:** None
**COVER LETTER:** Yes
**NUMBER OF COPIES:** Not given
**STYLE:** House
**FORMAT:** Standard
**ABSTRACT:** No
**LENGTH:** 3,000-4,000
**INSTRUCTION FORM:** Yes

**ACKNOWLEDGED:** Yes
**REVIEW PROCESS:** External reviewers
**NOTIFICATION TIME:** 1 month

**CRITICISM:** No

**ACCEPTANCE RATE:** 25%
**REVISION:** Varies
**EARLY PUBLICATION OPTION:** No
**COPYRIGHT POLICY:** Journal
**FEE:** $2.80 per page on publication
**REPRINTS:** 2 copies of issue
**PUBLICATION TIME LAG:** 2-3 years
**PROOFS:** Yes
**PAGE CHARGES:** No

**JOURNAL TITLE:** Sipapu

**SUBSCRIPTION ADDRESS:** Sipapu, Route 1, Box 216, Winters, CA 95694

**PRICE:** $4
**CIRCULATION:** 500
**AFFILIATION:** None
**INDEXED/ABSTRACTED:** CALL

**FREQUENCY:** Semiannual

**MANUSCRIPT ADDRESS:** Noel Peattie, Sipapu, Route 1, Box 216, Winters, CA 95694

**EDITORIAL POLICY:** A review and interview journal covering the dissent, alternative, small, independent, feminist, Third World, ecological, etc. press scene.

**AUDIENCE:** Librarians, editors and collectors

**PREFERRED TOPICS:** Interviews, descriptions of unusual libraries, coverage of conferences and meetings in the field.

**INAPPROPRIATE TOPICS:** Personal reminiscences, "poesy," personal "crank stuff, and unsolicited book reviews

**FEATURES:** Interviews in the field; please inquire before sending

**REVIEWS:** Yes

**STUDENT PAPERS:** No

**RESTRICTIONS:** None
**COVER LETTER:** Yes
**NUMBER OF COPIES:** 1
**STYLE:** No recommendation
**FORMAT:** Standard

**ABSTRACT:** No
**LENGTH:** 500
**INSTRUCTION FORM:** No, will send issue of magazine

**ACKNOWLEDGED:** Yes
**REVIEW PROCESS:** Not given

**NOTIFICATION TIME:** a few weeks

**CRITICISM:** No

**ACCEPTANCE RATE:** Varies
**REVISION:** Medium
**EARLY PUBLICATION OPTION:** No
**COPYRIGHT POLICY:** Publisher
**FEE:** $.04 a word
**REPRINTS:** Up to 10

**PUBLICATION TIME LAG:** Some months
**PROOFS:** Yes

**PAGE CHARGES:** Not given

**JOURNAL TITLE:** Society of Archivists Journal

**SUBSCRIPTION ADDRESS:** Mr. W. H. Baker, Society of Archivists, Gwent County Record Office, County Hall, Cwmbran, Gwent NP4 2XH, U.K.

**PRICE:** $10.50  **FREQUENCY:** Semiannual
**CIRCULATION:** 1,450
**AFFILIATION:** Society of Archivists
**INDEXED/ABSTRACTED:** LISA

**MANUSCRIPT ADDRESS:** Mrs. F. Strong, Society of Archivists Journal, South Cloister, Eton College, Windsor, Berkshire, SL4 6DB, England

**EDITORIAL POLICY:** To produce a professional journal covering practical and theoretical topics, for practicing archivists in Great Britain and the Commonwealth.

**AUDIENCE:** Professional archivists, historians

**PREFERRED TOPICS:** Archive administration, records management, conservation of documents, administrative history

**INAPPROPRIATE TOPICS:** Not given

**FEATURES:** Notes and News section--items of interest to archivists

**REVIEWS:** Yes  **STUDENT PAPERS:** No

**RESTRICTIONS:** None
**COVER LETTER:** Yes  **ABSTRACT:** No
**NUMBER OF COPIES:** 1  **LENGTH:** 6,000-8,000
**STYLE:** No recommendation  **INSTRUCTION FORM:** No
**FORMAT:** No recommendation

**ACKNOWLEDGED:** Yes  **NOTIFICATION TIME:** 1-2 weeks
**REVIEW PROCESS:** Not given

**CRITICISM:** Not normally

**ACCEPTANCE RATE:** Varies  **PUBLICATION TIME LAG:** 2-3 years
**REVISION:** Medium  **PROOFS:** Yes
**EARLY PUBLICATION OPTION:** No  **PAGE CHARGES:** No
**COPYRIGHT POLICY:** Author and publisher
**FEE:** None
**REPRINTS:** 6

JOURNAL TITLE: Southeastern Librarian

SUBSCRIPTION ADDRESS: Southeastern Library Association, P.O. Box 987, Tucker, GA 30084

PRICE: $10
CIRCULATION: 3,500
AFFILIATION: Southeastern Library Association
INDEXED/ABSTRACTED: LISA, LL
FREQUENCY: Quarterly

MANUSCRIPT ADDRESS: Leland M. Park, Southeastern Library, Davidson College Library, Davidson, NC 28036

EDITORIAL POLICY: Official journal of the Southeastern Library Association; articles about libraries or by librarians of the southeast are considered for publication.
AUDIENCE: Southeastern Library Association members, and members of the library profession
PREFERRED TOPICS: All types of articles pertaining to library operations and to the profession in general

INAPPROPRIATE TOPICS: Library histories which are not about libraries of the area

FEATURES: Ideas, Concepts, and Practices section

REVIEWS: Yes
STUDENT PAPERS: No

RESTRICTIONS: SELA members, writers about Southeastern libraries
COVER LETTER: Yes
NUMBER OF COPIES: 2
STYLE: Turabian
FORMAT: Standard
ABSTRACT: 50-100
LENGTH: Varies
INSTRUCTION FORM: No, given in journal

ACKNOWLEDGED: Yes
REVIEW PROCESS: Editorial board and external reviewers
CRITICISM: Usually
NOTIFICATION TIME: 1-2 weeks

ACCEPTANCE RATE: 50%
REVISION: Medium
EARLY PUBLICATION OPTION: No
COPYRIGHT POLICY: Not copyrighted
FEE: None
REPRINTS: 2 copies of issue
PUBLICATION TIME LAG: 1 year
PROOFS: No
PAGE CHARGES: No

JOURNAL TITLE: Special Collections

SUBSCRIPTION ADDRESS: Haworth Press, 28 East 22 Street, New York, NY  10010

PRICE: $85
CIRCULATION: New journal
AFFILIATION: None
INDEXED/ABSTRACTED: Not yet

FREQUENCY: Quarterly

MANUSCRIPT ADDRESS: Lee Ash, Special Collections, 66 Humiston Drive, Bethany, CT  06525

EDITORIAL POLICY: Articles by authoritative contributors offering major surveys of the history, content, and unusual resources in the larger collections in that field

AUDIENCE: Special collections, librarians, collectors, and scholars

PREFERRED TOPICS: Survey articles are prepared by invitation only; each issue focuses on a specific subject field

INAPPROPRIATE TOPICS: Not given

FEATURES: For each theme issue: articles on bibliographic control; lists of further collections in the same field; book review essays; guides to subject holdings in the U.S. and Canada

REVIEWS: Yes      STUDENT PAPERS: No

RESTRICTIONS: Not given
COVER LETTER: Yes
NUMBER OF COPIES: Not given
STYLE: Chicago
FORMAT: Standard

ABSTRACT: Not given
LENGTH: Not given
INSTRUCTION FORM: Yes

ACKNOWLEDGED: Yes (SASE)
REVIEW PROCESS: Editorial board and external reviewers

NOTIFICATION TIME: Not given

CRITICISM: Not given

ACCEPTANCE RATE:
REVISION: Not given
EARLY PUBLICATION OPTION: No
COPYRIGHT POLICY: Publisher
FEE: None
REPRINTS: 10

PUBLICATION TIME LAG: 6 months
PROOFS: Yes

PAGE CHARGES: No

JOURNAL TITLE: Special Libraries

SUBSCRIPTION ADDRESS: Special Libraries, 235 Park Avenue South, New York, NY 10003

PRICE: $26
CIRCULATION: 13,000
AFFILIATION: Special Libraries Association
INDEXED/ABSTRACTED: BPI, BRI, HA, HLI, ISA, LISA, LL, PAIS, SCI

FREQUENCY: 10 x a year

MANUSCRIPT ADDRESS: Nancy M. Viggiano, Special Libraries, Special Libraries, Association, 235 Park Avenue South, New York, NY 10003

EDITORIAL POLICY: Publishes material on all important subject areas and on all methods and techniques for "Putting Knowledge to Work."

AUDIENCE: Special Libraries Association members; library and information scientists and managers

PREFERRED TOPICS: New and developing areas of librarianship, information science and information technology, the administration, organization and cooperation of special libraries

INAPPROPRIATE TOPICS: Not given

FEATURES: Not given

REVIEWS: Yes

STUDENT PAPERS: No

RESTRICTIONS: None
COVER LETTER: Yes
NUMBER OF COPIES: 4
STYLE: House
FORMAT: House

ABSTRACT: 50-100
LENGTH: 5,000
INSTRUCTION FORM: Yes

ACKNOWLEDGED: Yes
REVIEW PROCESS: External reviewers

NOTIFICATION TIME: 1-3 months

CRITICISM: Sometimes

ACCEPTANCE RATE: 40%
REVISION: Medium
EARLY PUBLICATION OPTION: No
COPYRIGHT POLICY: Publisher
FEE: None
REPRINTS: 3

PUBLICATION TIME LAG: 4-6 months
PROOFS: Yes
PAGE CHARGES: No

JOURNAL TITLE: Special Libraries Association. Geography and Map Division. Bulletin
SUBSCRIPTION ADDRESS: Mrs. Kathleen I. Hickey, 9927 Edward Avenue, Bethesda, MD 20014

PRICE: $17
CIRCULATION: 900-1,000
AFFILIATION: SLA. Geography and Map Division
INDEXED/ABSTRACTED: BC, IH, LISA, LL

FREQUENCY: Quarterly

MANUSCRIPT ADDRESS: Mary Murphy, SLA Geography & Map Division Bulletin, 8102 Birnam Wood Drive, McLean, VA 22102

EDITORIAL POLICY: A medium of exchange of information, news and research in the field of geographic and cartographic bibliography, literature and libraries
AUDIENCE: Geography and map librarians
PREFERRED TOPICS: Original articles on research problems, technical services, and other aspects of cartographic and geographic literature, libraries, and collections are invited
INAPPROPRIATE TOPICS: Not given

FEATURES: Papers presented at Division meetings; Division news; lists of new maps, atlases, books, government publications of interest
REVIEWS: Yes
STUDENT PAPERS: No

RESTRICTIONS: None
COVER LETTER: Yes
NUMBER OF COPIES: 2
STYLE: No recommendation
FORMAT: No recommendation
ABSTRACT: No
LENGTH: 1,000-5,000
INSTRUCTION FORM: Not given

ACKNOWLEDGED: Yes
REVIEW PROCESS: Editor
NOTIFICATION TIME: 2-3 weeks

CRITICISM: No

ACCEPTANCE RATE: 95%
REVISION: Light
EARLY PUBLICATION OPTION: No
COPYRIGHT POLICY: Not copyrighted
FEE: None
REPRINTS: 2-4 copies of issue
PUBLICATION TIME LAG: 6-12 months
PROOFS: No
PAGE CHARGES: No

JOURNAL TITLE: Title Varies

SUBSCRIPTION ADDRESS: Title Varies, P.O. Box 704, Chapel Hill, NC 27514

PRICE: $5
CIRCULATION: 750
AFFILIATION: LUTFCSUSTC
INDEXED/ABSTRACTED: CALL

FREQUENCY: 6 x a year

MANUSCRIPT ADDRESS: David C. Taylor, Title Varies, P.O. Box 704, Chapel Hill, NC 27514

EDITORIAL POLICY: To publish articles concerning any aspect of serials publishing and library serials work

AUDIENCE: Librarians and publishers

PREFERRED TOPICS: Documented reports of title changes (both new "title variations" and summaries of the past records of frequent offenders)

INAPPROPRIATE TOPICS: Not given

FEATURES: Bibliography of serials and serials work; Title Change Hall of Fame

REVIEWS: Yes

STUDENT PAPERS: Yes

RESTRICTIONS: None
COVER LETTER: Yes
NUMBER OF COPIES: 1
STYLE: No recommendation
FORMAT: No recommendation

ABSTRACT: No
LENGTH: 1,000
INSTRUCTION FORM: Yes

ACKNOWLEDGED: Yes (SASE)
REVIEW PROCESS: Editor

NOTIFICATION TIME: 2 weeks

CRITICISM: Yes

ACCEPTANCE RATE: 60%
REVISION: Heavy
EARLY PUBLICATION OPTION: No
COPYRIGHT POLICY: Not copyrighted
FEE: None
REPRINTS: 5 copies of issue

PUBLICATION TIME LAG: 3 months
PROOFS: No

PAGE CHARGES: No

**JOURNAL TITLE:** Top of the News

**SUBSCRIPTION ADDRESS:** Subscription Services, American Library Association, 50 E. Huron Street, Chicago, IL 60611

**PRICE:** $15
**CIRCULATION:** 11,000
**AFFILIATION:** ALA, ALSC & YASD
**INDEXED/ABSTRACTED:** CIJE, LISA, LL

**FREQUENCY:** Quarterly

**MANUSCRIPT ADDRESS:** Audrey Eaglen, Top of the News, Cuyahoga County Public Library, 4510 Memphis Avenue, Cleveland, OH 44144

**EDITORIAL POLICY:** Serves as a vehicle for continuing education for librarians working with children and young adults

**AUDIENCE:** Children and young adult librarians, teachers of children's literature
**PREFERRED TOPICS:** Those that inform and aid working librarians; significant research

**INAPPROPRIATE TOPICS:** Academic minutiae

**FEATURES:** Two theme issues a year

**REVIEWS:** Yes

**STUDENT PAPERS:** No

**RESTRICTIONS:** None
**COVER LETTER:** Yes
**NUMBER OF COPIES:** 2
**STYLE:** House
**FORMAT:** House

**ABSTRACT:** No
**LENGTH:** 2,500-3,500
**INSTRUCTION FORM:** No

**ACKNOWLEDGED:** Yes
**REVIEW PROCESS:** Not given

**NOTIFICATION TIME:** 1 month

**CRITICISM:** No

**ACCEPTANCE RATE:** 90% solicited
**REVISION:** Medium
**EARLY PUBLICATION OPTION:** No
**COPYRIGHT POLICY:** Publisher
**FEE:** None
**REPRINTS:** 2 copies of issue

**PUBLICATION TIME LAG:** 3 months
**PROOFS:** No
**PAGE CHARGES:** No

JOURNAL TITLE: UNESCO Journal of Information Science, Librarianship and Archives Administration
SUBSCRIPTION ADDRESS: Office of the Unesco Press, UNESCO, 7 Place de Fontenoy, 75700 Paris, France

PRICE: $14.50
CIRCULATION:
AFFILIATION: UNESCO
INDEXED/ABSTRACTED: BS101, CC, CCA, CIJE, IB, IRB, LISA, LL
FREQUENCY: Quarterly

MANUSCRIPT ADDRESS: Mrs. Elizabeth Beyerly, UJISLAA, UNESCO, 7, Place de Fontenoy, 75700 Paris, France

EDITORIAL POLICY: Articles of international interest on theoretical and practical developments in the fields of information science, librarianship and archives administration
AUDIENCE: Information scientists, librarians, archivists
PREFERRED TOPICS: International, regional developments in UJISLAA's fields of competence
INAPPROPRIATE TOPICS: Descriptive articles about specific national library services
FEATURES: Biennial surveys of Unesco's information activities; standardization in the field of information; information networking.

REVIEWS: Yes
STUDENT PAPERS: Yes

RESTRICTIONS: Authors from Unesco's member states
COVER LETTER: Yes
NUMBER OF COPIES: 3
STYLE: House
FORMAT: Standard
ABSTRACT: 100-150
LENGTH: 3,000
INSTRUCTION FORM: Yes

ACKNOWLEDGED: Yes
REVIEW PROCESS: Editor and external reviewers
NOTIFICATION TIME: 6-8 weeks

CRITICISM: Yes

ACCEPTANCE RATE: 35-40%
REVISION: Heavy
EARLY PUBLICATION OPTION: No
COPYRIGHT POLICY: Publisher
FEE: $250-$300
REPRINTS: 25
PUBLICATION TIME LAG: 8-10 months
PROOFS: No
PAGE CHARGES: No

**JOURNAL TITLE:** The U*N*A*B*A*S*H*E*D Librarian

**SUBSCRIPTION ADDRESS:** The U*N*A*B*A*S*H*E*D Librarian, G.P.O. Box 2631, New York, NY 10001

**PRICE:** $15
**CIRCULATION:** Not given
**AFFILIATION:** None
**INDEXED/ABSTRACTED:** LL

**FREQUENCY:** Quarterly

**MANUSCRIPT ADDRESS:** Marvin H. Scilken, Unabashed Librarian, P.O. Box 2631, New York, NY 10001

**EDITORIAL POLICY:** The "how I run my library good" letter, welcomes items of a very practical nature and news of practices not in general use

**AUDIENCE:** Librarians

**PREFERRED TOPICS:** Short articles giving practical advice; descriptions of suggestions which require no (or minimal) research

**INAPPROPRIATE TOPICS:** None

**FEATURES:** Not given

**REVIEWS:** Not given

**STUDENT PAPERS:** Yes

**RESTRICTIONS:** None
**COVER LETTER:** No
**NUMBER OF COPIES:** 1
**STYLE:** No recommendation
**FORMAT:** No recommendation

**ABSTRACT:** No
**LENGTH:** Brief
**INSTRUCTION FORM:** No

**ACKNOWLEDGED:** No
**REVIEW PROCESS:** Editor

**NOTIFICATION TIME:** Varies

**CRITICISM:** Varies

**ACCEPTANCE RATE:** Varies
**REVISION:** Light
**EARLY PUBLICATION OPTION:** No
**COPYRIGHT POLICY:** Publisher
**FEE:** None
**REPRINTS:** 3 copies of issue

**PUBLICATION TIME LAG:** Varies
**PROOFS:** No

**PAGE CHARGES:** No

**JOURNAL TITLE:** Voice of Youth Advocates

**SUBSCRIPTION ADDRESS:** Voice of Youth Advocates, 10 Landing Lane #6M, New Brunswick, NJ 08901

**PRICE:** $15
**CIRCULATION:** 1,500
**AFFILIATION:** None
**INDEXED/ABSTRACTED:** Not

**FREQUENCY:** Bimonthly

**MANUSCRIPT ADDRESS:** Dorothy M. Broderick, Voice of Youth Advocates, 10 Landing Lane #6M, New Brunswick, NJ 08901

**EDITORIAL POLICY:** To demonstrate that library service to young adults in schools, public libraries and institutions has a valid theoretical basis.

**AUDIENCE:** Librarians, parents, academics, and youthworkers interested in adolescents

**PREFERRED TOPICS:** Almost anything on adolescents

**INAPPROPRIATE TOPICS:** Articles on children's literature and/or children

**FEATURES:** Lists, pathfinders, "Rx for Brainrot" (humor)

**REVIEWS:** Yes
**STUDENT PAPERS:** No

**RESTRICTIONS:** None
**COVER LETTER:** Yes
**NUMBER OF COPIES:** 1
**STYLE:** House
**FORMAT:** Standard

**ABSTRACT:** No
**LENGTH:** 2,000
**INSTRUCTION FORM:** Yes

**ACKNOWLEDGED:** Yes
**REVIEW PROCESS:** Editors

**NOTIFICATION TIME:** Up to a month

**CRITICISM:** Yes

**ACCEPTANCE RATE:** 50%
**REVISION:** Light
**EARLY PUBLICATION OPTION:** No
**COPYRIGHT POLICY:** Publisher
**FEE:** None
**REPRINTS:** 2

**PUBLICATION TIME LAG:** 6 months
**PROOFS:** No

**PAGE CHARGES:** No

**JOURNAL TITLE:** WLW Journal

**SUBSCRIPTION ADDRESS:** Women Library Workers Journal, P.O. Box 9052, Berkeley, CA 94709

**PRICE:** $15
**CIRCULATION:** 500
**AFFILIATION:** Women Library Workers
**INDEXED/ABSTRACTED:** Not

**FREQUENCY:** Bimonthly

**MANUSCRIPT ADDRESS:** Carol Starr, WLW Journal, P.O. Box 9052, Berkeley, CA 94709

**EDITORIAL POLICY:** A communications network and source of news and reviews of women's media for members of WLW and others interested in libraries and women's rights

**AUDIENCE:** WLW members and others interested in materials by/about women

**PREFERRED TOPICS:** Anything that ties women and libraries together

**INAPPROPRIATE TOPICS:** Not given

**FEATURES:** Regular reporting of women's actions and news as relates to libraries, reviews of media, reports and trends

**REVIEWS:** Yes
**STUDENT PAPERS:** Yes

**RESTRICTIONS:** None
**COVER LETTER:** Yes
**NUMBER OF COPIES:** 2
**STYLE:** Chicago
**FORMAT:** Standard

**ABSTRACT:** No
**LENGTH:** 500-1,000
**INSTRUCTION FORM:** No

**ACKNOWLEDGED:** Yes (SASE)
**REVIEW PROCESS:** Editorial board

**NOTIFICATION TIME:** 3 weeks

**CRITICISM:** If time permits

**ACCEPTANCE RATE:** 80%
**REVISION:** Medium
**EARLY PUBLICATION OPTION:** No
**COPYRIGHT POLICY:** Author and publisher
**FEE:** Write for information
**REPRINTS:** 2 copies of issue

**PUBLICATION TIME LAG:** 1-3 months
**PROOFS:** No
**PAGE CHARGES:** No

JOURNAL TITLE: Western Association of Map Libraries. Information Bulletin
SUBSCRIPTION ADDRESS: Western Association of Map Libraries, c/o Stanley D. Stevens, Treasurer, University Library, University of California, Santa Cruz, CA 95064

PRICE: $10
FREQUENCY: 3 x a year
CIRCULATION: 400
AFFILIATION: Western Association of Map Libraries
INDEXED/ABSTRACTED: AC, GAG, LISA, LL

MANUSCRIPT ADDRESS: Stanley D. Stevens, Western Association of Map Libraries, Information Bulletin, University Library, University of California at Santa Cruz, Santa Cruz, CA 95064
EDITORIAL POLICY: Emphasizes the interests of the WAML membership, which is to encourage high standards in every phase of organization and administration of map libraries
AUDIENCE: Librarians with responsibility for maps
PREFERRED TOPICS: Articles, book reviews, citations of new maps and atlases, antiquarian maps and atlases, history of cartography, modern collections of maps and atlases; preservation of maps
INAPPROPRIATE TOPICS: None

FEATURES: Citations of "New Mapping of Western North America," and "Publications of Relevance"

REVIEWS: Yes
STUDENT PAPERS: Yes

RESTRICTIONS: None
COVER LETTER: Yes
NUMBER OF COPIES: 2
STYLE: Under review
FORMAT: Standard
ABSTRACT: 100-150
LENGTH: 10 pages
INSTRUCTION FORM: Yes

ACKNOWLEDGED: Yes
REVIEW PROCESS: Editorial board
NOTIFICATION TIME: 1 week

CRITICISM: Yes

ACCEPTANCE RATE: 95%
REVISION: Light
EARLY PUBLICATION OPTION: No
PUBLICATION TIME LAG: 2 months
PROOFS: Yes
PAGE CHARGES: No
COPYRIGHT POLICY: Publisher, author may copyright his own work
FEE: None
REPRINTS: None

JOURNAL TITLE: Wilson Library Bulletin

SUBSCRIPTION ADDRESS: H. W. Wilson Company, 950 University Avenue, Bronx, NY 10452

PRICE: $17
CIRCULATION: 27,000
AFFILIATION: None
INDEXED/ABSTRACTED: AHL, BRI, CBRC, EdI, HA, LISA, LL, PPI

FREQUENCY: 10 x a year

MANUSCRIPT ADDRESS: Milo Nelson, Wilson Library Bulletin, H. W. Wilson Company, 950 University Avenue, Bronx, NY 10452

EDITORIAL POLICY: A general interest library publication that, in a time of accelerated technological change, strives to remind its readers of the humanistic basis of the profession

AUDIENCE: School, public, academic and special librarians; educators and information specialists

PREFERRED TOPICS: Architecture, automation, library history, administration, public relations, networks, and bibliography

INAPPROPRIATE TOPICS: Articles concerned with the image of librarians and librarianship

FEATURES: Dateline-Washington; Government Publications

REVIEWS: Yes

STUDENT PAPERS: No

RESTRICTIONS: None
COVER LETTER: Yes
NUMBER OF COPIES: 2
STYLE: MLA
FORMAT: Standard

ABSTRACT: No
LENGTH: 2,400
INSTRUCTION FORM: Not given

ACKNOWLEDGED: Yes
REVIEW PROCESS: Editors

NOTIFICATION TIME: 60 days

CRITICISM: On occasion

ACCEPTANCE RATE: 90% commissioned
REVISION: Medium
EARLY PUBLICATION OPTION: No
COPYRIGHT POLICY: Author and publisher
FEE: $100 and up
REPRINTS: 6 copies of issue

PUBLICATION TIME LAG: 60-90 days
PROOFS: No
PAGE CHARGES: No

## OTHER JOURNALS

Despite our best efforts, which included several mailings and in some cases telephone calls, a number of editors whose journals would seem to warrant inclusion did not respond to our requests for information or supplied information that was too incomplete to enable us to provide a complete entry for their journal. In a few cases, the editors indicated that the journal was undergoing a change of editors, or a change of editorial policy, which meant that the available information would no longer be relevant by the time this guide was published. Finally, in a few cases we were aware of new journals that were in the process of being established for which it was simply too early for the editor and/or publisher to provide the information requested. Rather than providing partial information in the main section of this guide, or omitting those journals altogether, we have elected to provide the following brief listing of other journals. This listing provides only the title of the journal and the best currently available editorial address based on information supplied by the editor or publisher, from current periodical directories, or from an examination of a current issue of the journal. All of these titles have been included in the index. For prospective authors interested in contributing to any of these journals we would suggest that a letter of inquiry asking for up-to-date information about the editorial and publishing practices of the journal be addressed to the editor along with an indication of the subject of the article that the prospective author has written or intends to write.

*AB Bookman's Weekly*
  Jacob L. Chernofsky
  P.O. Box AB
  Clifton, NJ 07105

*ECT*
  Robert Heinich
  Association for Educational Communication & Technology
  1126 16th Street, N.W.
  Washington, DC 20036

*Antiquarian Book Monthly Review*
  Joanna Dodsworth
  ABMR Publications Limited
  52 St. Clement's Street
  Oxford OX4 1AG, England

*Art Libraries Journal*
  Sonia French
  15 Fordhouse Road
  Bromsgrove, Worcs. B60 2LU, England

## 174 / Other Journals

*Assistant Librarian*
Robert N. Froud
West Norwood Library
1 Norwood High Street
London SE27, England

*Bibliographical Society of America, Papers*
William B. Todd
Parlin Hall 110
University of Texas
Austin, TX 78712

*Book Collector*
Nicolas Barker
Collector Limited
3 Bloomsbury Place
London WC1A 2QA, England

*Book Collectors Market*
Denis Carbonneau
Moretus Press
363 7th Avenue
New York, NY 10001

*Computing Reviews*
Arthur Blum
Association for Computing Machinery
1133 Avenue of the Americas
New York, NY 10036

*Dikta*
Patricia Ward Salas
P.O. Box 2299
Daytona Beach, FLA 32105

*Educational Media International*
Jennifer Suthrell
254 Belsize Road
London NW6, England

*Federal Libraries*
David Hoyt
Federal Library Committee
Library of Congress
Washington, DC 20540

*Government Publications Review*
Bernard M. Fry
Graduate Library School
Indiana University
Bloomington, IND 47401

*Herald of Library Science*
P.N. Kaula
P.K. Endowment for Library and Information Science
C-1 Banaras Hindu University
Varanasi 221005, India

*IATUL Proceedings*
Nancy Fjällbrant
Library
Chalmers University of Technology
S-40220
Gothenburg S, Sweden

*INSPEL*
Paul Kaegbein
Bibliothekar-Lehrinstitut des Landes Nordrhein-Westfalen
Universitätstrasse 33
D-5000 Cologne 41 (Lindenthal), West Germany

*Information Processing and Management*
Bernard M. Fry
Graduate Library School
Indiana University
Bloomington, IND 47401

*Information Sciences*
 John M. Richardson
 North American Rockwell
  Corporation
 Science Center
 Aerospace and Systems Group
 1049 Camino Dos Rios
 Thousand Oaks, CA 91360

*Information Systems*
 Hans-Jochen Schneider
 c/o Pergamon Press, Inc.
 Maxwell House
 Fairview Park
 Elmsford, NY 10523

*Information Technology and Human Affairs*
 T.D. Sterling
 c/o Pergamon Press, Inc.
 Maxwell House
 Fairview Park
 Elmsford, NY 1052

*Interface*
 Linda H. Mielke
 Special Community Services
 Division of Library Development
  & Services
 Maryland State Department of
  Education
 Baltimore, MD 21240

*International Journal of Archives*
 James E. O'Neill
 U.S. National Archives and
  Records Service
 8th Street & Pennsylvania Avenue,
  N.W.
 Washington, DC 20408

*International Journal of Law Libraries*
 Klaus Menzinger
 Director, Bibliothek fur
  Rechtswissenschaft der
  Universitat Freiburg
 Werthmannplatz 1, 7800 Frieburg
  i. Br., W. Germany

*International Library Review*
 George Chandler
 c/o Academic Press
 111 Fifth Avenue
 New York, NY 10003

*Interracial Books for Children*
 Bradford Chambers
 Council on Interracial Books for
  Children, Inc.
 1841 Broadway
 New York, NY 10023

*Journal of Cybernetics and Information Science*
 Kumpati S. Narendra
 Department of Engineering and
  Applied Science
 Yale University
 New Haven, CT 06520

*Journal of Informatics*
 B.C. Brookes
 School of Library, Archive and
  Information Studies
 University College
 Gower Street
 London, WC1, England

*Journal of Information Science*
 A. Gilchrist
 Institute of Information Scientists
 Harvest House
 62 London Road
 Reading, Berkshire RG1 5AS,
  England

*Library*
Peter Davison
Oxford University Press
Press Road
Neasden, London NW10 ODD,
England

*Library Acquisitions*
Scott Bullard
Head, Acquisition Department
University Libraries
University of Louisville
Louisville, KY 40208

*Library Association Record*
R.M. Walter
Library Association
7 Ridgmount Street
London WC1E 7AE, England

*Library-College Experimenter*
Sandra Sheppard
Box 956
Norman, OK 73070

*Library Connection*
James Godfrey
Rye Country Day School
Boston Post Road & Cedar Street
Rye, NY 10580

*Library Review*
J.D. Hendry & Graham Jones
Holmes McDougall Limited
10/12 York Street
Glasgow G2 8LG, Scotland

*Library Science with a Slant to Documentation*
A. Neelameghan
Sarada Ranganathan Endowment
  for Library Science
DRTC, 31 Church Street
Cantonment, Bangalore 560001,
  India

*Libri*
Preben Kikegaard
Director, Royal School of
  Librarianship
6 Birketinget
DH-2300 Copenhagen S, Denmark
58 60 66

*Moccasin Telegraph*
Linda McCoy
Canadian School Library
  Association
151 Sparks Street
Ottawa K1P SE 3, Canada

*Musikbibliothek Aktuell*
Hans Vetterlein
Deutscher Bibliotheksverband
  E.V.
Fehrbelliner Platz 3
1000 Berlin 31, W. Germany

*National Preservation Report*
Imre T. Jamry
National Preservation Program
  Office
Library of Congress
Washington, DC 20540

*Picturescope*
Grace E. Evans
6307 Bannockburn Drive
Washington, DC 20034

*Publishers' Weekly*
John F. Baker
R.R. Bowker
1180 Avenue of the Americas
New York, NY 10036

*Research in Librarianship*
Edward R. Reid-Smith
P.O. Box 744
Wagga Wagga, New South Wales
  2650, Australia

*Restaurator*
  Poul A. Christiansen
  University Library
  Scientific and Medical
    Department
  49 Nörre Alle
  DK 2200
  Copenhagen N, Denmark

*School Media Quarterly*
  Jack R. Luskay
  School of Library Science
  Clarion State College
  Clarion, PA 16214

*Sci-Tech News*
  Susan Crowe
  Aerospace Corporation
  P.O. Box 92957
  Los Angeles, CA 92957

*Urban Academic Librarian*
  Marguerite Iskendarian
  Brooklyn College Library
  Bedford Avenue & Avenue H
  Brooklyn, NY 11210

# ASSOCIATION, KEYWORD, AND SUBJECT INDEX

Journals are listed in this index under the name of the association or institution with which they are affiliated, as well as under key words within their title and under subject.

## A

*Academic Libraries*
  Choice, 58
  College & Research Libraries, 64
  College & Research Libraries
    News, 65
  Journal of Academic
    Librarianship, 93
  Learning Today, 109
  Outlook on Research Libraries, 138
*Acquisitions*
  Choice, 58
  Collection Building, 62
  Collection Management, 63
  Legal Reference Services
    Quarterly, 110
  Library Resources . . . , 120
  Microform Review, 130
  Reference Book Review, 147
  Reference Services Review, 148
  Serials Review, 156
*Administration*
  Conservation Administration
    News, 67
  Journal of Library
    Administration, 100
  UNESCO Journal of
    Information . . . , 167
*Advocates*, Voice of Youth, 169
*Agricultural Librarianship*
  International Assn. of Agricultural
    Librarians & Documentalists.
    Quarterly Bulletin, 89
*Alternative Librarianship*
  Emergency Librarian, 75
  Librarians for Social Change, 111
  SRRT Newsletter, 151

*Alternative Librarianship (cont.)*
  Sipapu, 159
  Unabashed Librarian, 168
  Voice of Youth Advocates, 169
  WLW Journal, 172
*American Assn. of Law Libraries*
  Law Library Journal, 108
*American Chemical Society*
  Journal of Chemical Information, 94
*American Library Assn.*
  American Libraries, 38
  Choice, 58
  College & Research Libraries, 64
  College & Research Libraries
    News, 65
  Documents to the People, 71
*American Library Assn.*
  Footnotes, 71
  Journal of Library Automation, 102
  Library Resources . . . , 120
  Public Libraries, 143
  RQ, 145
  RTSD Newsletter, 146
  Top of the News, 166
*American Society of Indexers*
  Indexer, 85
*Archives*
  American Archivist, 36
  Archivaria, 43
  Archives, 44
  Library and Archival Security, 112
  Midwestern Archivist, 131
  Society of Archivists. Journal, 160
  UNESCO Journal of
    Information . . . , 167
*Artis Musicae*, Fontes, 78
*Aslib* Program, 142
*Assn. for Computers & the Humanities*
  Computers and the Humanities, 66

## Association, Keyword, and Subject Index / 179

*Assn. for Educational Communication & Technology*, Instructional Innovator, 88
*Assn. for Library Service to Children*
  Top of the News, 166
*Assn. for Systems Management*
  Journal of Systems Management, 106
*Assn. Internationale des Bibliotheques Musicales*
  Brio, 47
  Fontes Artis Musicae, 78
*Assn. of American Library Schools*
  Journal of Education for Librarianship, 98
*Assn. of Canadian Archivists*
  Archivaria, 43
*Assn. of College & Research Libraries*
  Choice, 58
  College & Research Libraries, 64
  College & Research Libraries News, 65
*Assn. of Jewish Libraries*
  AJL Bulletin, 33
*Atlantic Provinces Library Assn.*
  APLA Bulletin, 34
*Australian Society of Indexers*
  Indexer, 85
*Austrian Society for Cybernetic Studies*
  Journal of Cybernetics, 96
*Automation*
  Information Retrieval & Library Automation, 87
  Journal of Library Automation, 102
  Program, 142

### B

*Bible Study*, AJL Bulletin, 33
*Bibliography*, Bulletin of Bibliography, 48
*Book Collecting*, Private Library, 141
*Book Reviewing*
  Choice, 85
  Legal Reference Services Quarterly, 110
  Reference Book Review, 147
  Reference Services Review, 148
  Serials Review, 156

*British Library. Research & Development Department,* Library Management News, 116
*British Records Assn.*, Archives, 44

### C

*Canadian Assn. for Information Science*
  Canadian Journal of Information Science, 51
*Canadian Library Assn.*
  Canadian Library Journal, 52
*Cataloging*
  Annals of Library Science . . . , 42
  Cataloging & Classification Quarterly, 53
  Catalogue & Index, 54
  International Cataloging, 90
  Library Resources . . . , 120
  RTSD Newsletter, 146
*Cataloguing and Indexing Group*
  Catalogue & Index, 54
*Catholic Library Assn.*
  Catholic Library World, 55
*Change,* Librarians for Social, 111
*Chemical Information and Computer Sciences,* Journal of, 94
*Chicanos,* Amoxcalli Newsletter, 41
*Children and Young Adult Services*
  Emergency Librarian, 75
  Top of the News, 166
  Voice of Youth Advocates, 169
*Children's Literature*
  Canadian Children's Literature, 50
  Children's Literature, 56
  Children's Literature in Education, 57
  Horn Book, 80
  The Lion and the Unicorn, 123
  Phaedrus, 140
  Signal, 158
*Children's Literature Assn.*
  Children's Literature, 56
*Chinese American Librarians Assn.*
  Journal of Library . . . , 101
*Christian Librarians' Fellowship*
  Christian Librarian, 59
*Church and Synagogue Libraries Assn.*
  Church and Synagogue Libraries, 60
*Classification*
  Annals of Library Science . . . , 42
  Cataloguing & Classification

*Classification (cont.)*
   Quarterly, 53
   Catalogue & Index, 54
   Classification Society Bulletin, 61
   International Classification, 91
*Committee on Classification Research*
   International Classification, 91
*Communication*, IEEE Transactions on Professional, 82
*Communication Studies*, Journal of Research, 105
*Computer Sciences*
   Journal of Chemical Information . . . , 94
   Journal of Computer . . . , 95
*Council on Library/Media Technical Assistants*, COLT Newsletter, 49

### D

*Data Processing Management Assn.*
   Data Management, 69

### E

*Education*
   Children's Literature in Education, 57
   Education Libraries, 73
   Educational Technology, 74
   Media & Methods, 127
*Education Div. Special Libraries Assn.*
   Education Libraries, 73
*Education for Librarianship,* Journal, 98
*Educational Film Library Assn.*
   Sightlines, 157
*Educational Technology*
   Educational Technology, 74
   Film Library Quarterly, 76
   Instructional Innovator, 88
   Media & Methods, 127
   Sightlines, 157

### F

*Film Library Information Council*
   Film Library Quarterly, 76

### G

*Geography and Map Div. Special Libraries Assn.* Bulletin, 164

*Gesellschaft fur klassifikation e. V.*
   International Classification, 91
*Government Documents*
   Documents to the People, 71

### H

*History,* Journal of Library, 103
*History,* Library, 113
*History Review,* Library, 114

### I

*Indexing*
   Catalogue & Index, 54
   Indexer, 85
   International Cataloguing, 90
*Indian National Scientific Documentation Centre.* Annals of Library Science . . . , 42
*Information Science*
   ASIS. Bulletin, 39
   ASIS. Journal, 40
   Annals of Library Science . . . , 42
   Canadian Journal of Information . . . , 51
   IEEE Transactions on Information Theory, 81
   Information Hotline, 86
   Information Retrieval . . . , 87
   International Forum on Information . . . , 92
   Journal of Chemical Information . . . , 94
   Journal of Computer and Information . . . , 95
   Journal of Cybernetics, 96
   Journal of Documentation, 97
   Journal of Library . . . , 101
   Methods of Information in Medicine, 129
   UNESCO Journal of Information . . . , 167
*Information Theory Group. IEEE*
   IEEE Transactions on Information . . . , 81
*Institute of Electrical and Electronics Engineers,* IEEE Transactions on Information Theory, 81
   IEEE Transactions on Professional . . . , 82
*Interlibrary Loan,* Just b'TWX Us, 107

Association, Keyword, and Subject Index / 181

*International Agency for Research in Library History,* Library History Review, 114
*International and Comparative Librarianship Group,* Focus on International and Comparative . . . , 77
*International Assn. of Agricultural Librarians & Documentalists,* Quarterly Bulletin, 89
*International Assn. of Music Libraries*
Brio, 47
Fontes Artis Musicae, 78
*International Federation for Documentation,* International Classification, 91
International Forum on Information . . . , 92
*International Federation of Library Assns. & Institutions*
IFLA Journal, 83
International Cataloguing, 90
International Classification, 91
*International Micrographic Congress*
IMC Journal, 84
*International Office for Universal Bibliographic Control*
International Cataloguing, 90
International Classification, 91
*Internationalen Vereinigung der Musikbibliothe*
Brio, 47
Fontes Artis Musicae, 78

J

*Jewish Libraries*
AJL Bulletin, 33
Church & Synagogue Libraries, 60
Journal of the American Society for Information Science, 40
Journal of the Assn. for Recorded Sound, 45
Journal of the Society of Archivists, 160
*Junior Members Roundtable,* Footnotes, 79

L

*Law Librarianship*
Law Library Journal, 108

Legal Reference Services Quarterly, 110
*Library Administration,* Journal of Library Management News, 116
*Library and Information Technology Assn.,* Journal of Library Automation, 102
*Library Assn.*
Catalogue & Index, 54
Focus on International . . . , 77
Journal of Librarianship, 99
Library History, 113
*Library Automation*
Information Retrieval & Library . . . , 87
Journal of Library Automation, 102
*Library Binding Institute*
Library Scene, 121
*Library-College Associates*
Learning Today, 109
*Library Education*
Journal of Education for Librarianship, 98
*Library History,* Journal of, 103
*Library History Group* Library History, 113
*Library Research*
Journal of Research Communication . . . , 105
Library Quarterly, 118
Library Research, 119

M

*Management,* Collection, 63
*Management,* Data, 69
*Management,* Journal of Systems, 106
*Management News,* Library, 116
*Map Librarianship*
Special Libraries Assn. Geography and Map Division, Bulletin, 164
Western Assn. of Map Libraries, Information Bulletin, 170
*Medical Librarianship*
Medical Library Assn. Bulletin, 128
Methods of Information in Medicine, 129
*Micrographics*
IMC Journal, 84
Journal of Micrographics, 104
Microform Review, 130
Reprographics Quarterly, 149

*Middle East Librarians Assn.*
  MELA Notes, 124
*Midwest Archives Conference*
  Midwestern Archivist, 131
*Modern Language Assn.*
  Children's Literature, 56
*Mountain Plains Library Assn.*
  MPLA Newsletter, 125
*Music Librarianship*
  Association for Recorded Sound
    Collection, Journal, 45
  Brio, 47
  Fontes Artis Musicae, 78
  Notes, 134
*Music Library Assn.*, Notes, 134

## N

*National Libraries Assn.*
  NLA Newsletter, 132
*National Micrographics Assn.*
  Journal of Micrographics, 104
*Networks*
  Information Hotline, 86
  Resource Sharing & Library
    Networks, 150

## O

*Online Services*
  Database Magazine, 70
  Information Hotline, 86
  Online Magazine, 136
  Online Review, 137

## P

*Pacific Northwest Library Assn.*
  PNLA Quarterly, 139
*Preservation*
  Conservation Administration
    News, 67
  Library and Archival Security, 112
  Library Scene, 121
*Private Libraries Assn.*
  Private Library, 141
*Professional Communication Society.*
  *IEEE,* IEEE Transactions on
    Professional Communication, 82
*Public Library Assn.* Public
  Libraries, 143
*Public Relations.* Library PR News, 117

## R

*Reference and Adult Services Div. ALA*
  RQ, 145
*Reference Services,* Legal
  Quarterly, 110
*Reforma. El Paso Chapter*
  Amoxcalli Newsletter, 41
*Religious Librarianship*
  AJL Bulletin, 33
  Catholic Library World, 55
  Christian Librarian, 59
  Church & Synagogue Libraries, 60
  Media, 126
*Resources & Technical Services Div.*
  Library Resources &
    Technical . . . , 120
  RTSD Newsletter, 146
*Reviews*
  Reference Book Review, 147
  Reference Services Review, 148
  Serials Review, 156

## S

*School Libraries*
  Emergency Librarian, 75
  School Librarian, 152
  School Library Journal, 153
*School Library Assn.,* School
  Librarian, 152
*Science Librarianship*
  Science & Technology Libraries, 154
*Serials*
  Serials Librarian, 155
  Serials Review, 156
  Title Varies, 165
*Social Change,* Librarians for, 111
*Social Responsibilities Round Table*
  SRRT Newsletter, 151
*Social Sciences*
  Behavioral & Social Sciences . . . , 46
*Societe Canadienne pour L'Analyse de
  Documentation,* Indexer, 85
*Society of American Archivists*
  American Archivist, 36
*Society of Indexers,* Indexer, 85
*Southeastern Library Assn.*
  Southeastern Librarian, 161
*Special Libraries*
  Aslib Proceedings, 35
  Program, 142

*Special Libraries (cont.)*
   Special Libraries, 163
*Special Libraries Assn.*
   Education Libraries, 73
   Special Libraries, 163
*Special Libraries Assn. Geography and Map Div.*, Bulletin, 164
*Sunday School Board of the Southern Baptist Convention*, Media, 126
*Synagogue Libraries*
   Church & Synagogue Libraries, 60
*Technical Assistants* COLT Newsletter, 49
*Technical Services*
   Library Resources & Technical . . . , 120
   RTSD Newsletter, 146
*Technology*
   Educational Technology, 74
   Science & Technology Libraries, 154

## U

*Unicorn*, The Lion and the, 123
*University of Chicago. Graduate Library School*, Library Quarterly, 118
*University of Illinois. Graduate School of Library Science*
   Library Trends, 122
   Occasional Papers, 135
*University of Wyoming. Libraries*
   Conservation Administration News, 67

## W

*Women Library Workers*, WLW Journal, 172

## Y

*Young Adult Services Div. ALA*
   Top of the News, 166
*Youth Advocates*, Voice of, 169

For Product Safety Concerns and Information please contact our EU representative  GPSR@taylorandfrancis.com
Taylor & Francis Verlag GmbH, Kaufingerstraße 24, 80331 München, Germany

www.ingramcontent.com/pod-product-compliance
Lightning Source LLC
Chambersburg PA
CBHW070613300426
44113CB00010B/1519